Your Complete Guide to

Early
Retirement

A Step-by-Step Plan for
Making It Happen

By Sandy Baker

YOUR COMPLETE GUIDE TO EARLY RETIREMENT:
A Step-by-Step Plan for Making It Happen

Copyright © 2007 by Atlantic Publishing Group, Inc.
1405 SW 6th Ave. • Ocala, Florida 34471 • 800-814-1132 • 352-622-1875–Fax
Web site: **www.atlantic-pub.com** • E-mail: sales@atlantic-pub.com
SAN Number: 268-1250

ISBN-13: 978-0-910627-93-1   ISBN-10: 0-910627-93-2

Baker, Sandy Ann, 1976-
  Your complete guide to early retirement : a step-by-step plan for making it happen / by Sandra Ann Baker.
    p. cm.
Includes indexes.
ISBN 13: 978-0-910627-93-1 (alk. paper)
ISBN 10: 0-910627-93-2 (alk. paper)
  1. Early retirement--United States--Planning--Handbooks, manuals, etc. I. Title.
  HD7110.5.U6B35 2007
  332.024'0140973--dc22
                        2007035693

EDITOR: Tracie Kendziora • tkendziora@atlantic-pub.com
INTERIOR DESIGN: Vickie Taylor • vtaylor@atlantic-pub.com
COVER DESIGN & PROOFREADER: Angela Adams • aadams@atlantic-pub.com

Printed on Recycled Paper

Printed in the United States

We recently lost our beloved pet "Bear," who was not only
our best and dearest friend but also the "Vice President of
Sunshine" here at Atlantic Publishing. He did not receive
a salary but worked tirelessly 24 hours a day to please
his parents. Bear was a rescue dog that turned around
and showered myself, my wife Sherri, his grandparents
Jean, Bob and Nancy and every person and animal he met
(maybe not rabbits) with friendship and love. He made a
lot of people smile every day.

We wanted you to know that a portion of the profits of this
book will be donated to The Humane Society of
the United States.

–Douglas & Sherri Brown

THE HUMANE SOCIETY
OF THE UNITED STATES©

The human-animal bond is as old as human history. We cherish our animal companions for their unconditional affection and acceptance. We feel a thrill when we glimpse wild creatures in their natural habitat or in our own backyard.

Unfortunately, the human-animal bond has at times been weakened. Humans have exploited some animal species to the point of extinction.

The Humane Society of the United States makes a difference in the lives of animals here at home and worldwide. The HSUS is dedicated to creating a world where our relationship with animals is guided by compassion. We seek a truly humane society in which animals are respected for their intrinsic value, and where the human-animal bond is strong.

Want to help animals? We have plenty of suggestions. Adopt a pet from a local shelter, join The Humane Society and be a part of our work to help companion animals and wildlife. You will be funding our educational, legislative, investigative and outreach projects in the U.S. and across the globe.

Or perhaps you'd like to make a memorial donation in honor of a pet, friend or relative? You can through our Kindred Spirits program. And if you'd like to contribute in a more structured way, our Planned Giving Office has suggestions about estate planning, annuities, and even gifts of stock that avoid capital gains taxes.

Maybe you have land that you would like to preserve as a lasting habitat for wildlife. Our Wildlife Land Trust can help you. Perhaps the land you want to share is a backyard—that's enough. Our Urban Wildlife Sanctuary Program will show you how to create a habitat for your wild neighbors.

So you see, it's easy to help animals. And The HSUS is here to help.

The Humane Society of the United States
2100 L Street NW
Washington, DC 20037
202-452-1100
www.hsus.org

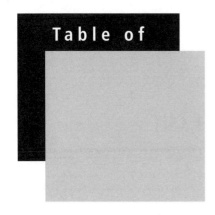

Table of

CONTENTS

CHAPTER 3: IT IS NOT A SIMPLE CUT AND DRY DEAL 55

CHAPTER 4: LIFE CHANGES IN RETIREMENT AND BEFORE 69

CHAPTER 5: HAVING MONEY AND BEING WEALTHY 83

CHAPTER 6: WEALTH — YOU CAN GET THERE 97

CHAPTER 7: YOU ARE A MILLIONAIRE IN TRAINING! 129

CHAPTER 8: GET YOUR PLAN TOGETHER 141

CHAPTER 9: THE RIGHT INVESTMENT STRATEGY FOR YOU 165

CHAPTER 12: IRAS MUST BE UNDERSTOOD 227

CHAPTER 13: YOUR ESTATE PLAN 255

CONCLUSION 271

BIBLIOGRAPHY 277

AUTHOR DEDICATION AND BIOGRAPHY 278

INTRODUCTION

Retiring early used to be something that you planned to do. When you got your first job after college, you planned to take the business world by storm. You planned to make your first million by the time you were 25 and to be well on your way to wealth before any of your friends.

Or perhaps you spent those first years planning how you would get a good job and live a good life with very few lofty goals. You wanted a simple life with a family, good friends, and maybe a few children.

Now, you are working every day all day and you find yourself without a lot of dreams left for the future. You know that you can definitely keep going on the same path and keep living the same life. But why not ask yourself, "What if...."

What if you could retire early? What if in five, ten, or more years you could tell your boss that you quit and plan to take a trip around the world with your spouse? What if you could finally stop working overtime and holidays just to have a little extra money in your pocket? What if you could dream about doing anything and having anything you want without thinking it is a lofty dream?

When you learn the solid method to achieving the goals that you have in terms of your finances, you can achieve anything, including retiring early. There are many things that go into everyday life, and even if right now you are thinking there is no chance of making ends meet, you can change your life for the better, and you can make all of those "what if" plans come true.

There are several key things to making this happen. To retire early, you need to change your current way of living and spending. You will need to remove debt from your name (but no matter how large it is, we will show you how to get rid of it). You also need to accumulate capital, the right way, so that you have what you need to live off of. Finally, you need to learn how to invest wisely so that each dollar you invest is a well invested dollar that will bring you the type and amount of return you are interested in.

In this book, you will learn how to do these things and much more. By providing you with the information you need, in a simple and step-by-step approach, you can and will find yourself able to retire early.

Learn how to finally walk away from your dead end job and into the life that you were meant to live.

CHAPTER 1

WHAT DOES RETIREMENT MEAN TO YOU?

The process of retiring is one that takes careful consideration. No matter what part of the road to retirement you are on, you can and will find an ultimate end result if you use the tools that are given to you here. One of the first things you need to develop and carefully consider is what retirement means to you and why you want to retire in the first place.

Perhaps you want to stop for a second and contemplate exactly what retirement means to you. When you look at your paycheck, you see that there are deductions taken out. Social Security is deducted as a promise to give you back something when you do stop working. You have Medicare, which you are funding to help provide for your medical needs when you do retire. The problem, though, is that those funds are not enough. On top of that, it is now commonly thought that the Baby Boomer generation will wipe out Social Security for younger generations.

The point here is simple. For most people, Social Security is not enough to continue to fund the life style to which they are accustomed. That said, you may want to consider exactly what it means to you to have the ability to carry on at least the same life style, if not better. It is costly, without a doubt.

The good news is that anyone at any age can take what they have and develop a plan for retirement. This means that if you are 22 you have more time, but it also means that if you are quickly approaching 50 you too can make wise decisions that will completely change your life. Furthermore, you will be able to retire faster.

ASKING THE HARD QUESTIONS

The intention of this book is to force you to ask many hard questions and encourage you to write down your goals for the future and the age by which you want to achieve these goals. Having a written plan will not only increase the likelihood of achieving your goals, but will also help you adapt to any major life changes that interrupt your progress. Later, we will go into more detail about the changes that could affect your plans for early retirement and how to deal with them as they arise. For now, consider the following questions seriously, and write specific and detailed responses to those that pertain to your personal situation. They are meant to help you formulate a clear plan for your retirement by identifying what is important to you.

How long of a retirement are you planning?

- How old are you now?

- At what age do you wish to retire?

- How long can you expect to live?

What will you do during retirement?

- Will you travel?

- Will you begin a new career?

- Will you continue working your current job on a smaller scale?

- Will you go back to school?

- Will you volunteer?

How might your family affect your plans for early retirement?

- Are you near your children or other important family members?

- Are you sending children to college?

- Are you taking care of older parents?

- Will your spouse continue to work after you retire?

- How often do you plan to visit family?

- Will they have somewhere to stay when they visit you?

- As you age, will you need help from family? Would you be willing to move closer to them for this purpose?

How might your health affect your plans for early retirement?

- Do you have any current health concerns that may present a problem for you down the road?

- Does your family have a history of certain health conditions?

- How might those specific concerns, if any, affect your finances?

- Can you alter your life style to prevent specific health concerns from becoming a problem in the future?

- How can your doctor help you prepare for future health concerns?

Where will you live?

- Will you live where you live now?

- Will your home be paid for by the time you retire?

- Are you planning on relocating in retirement?

Will you travel?

- How often will you travel?

- Where will you travel?

- What will be the cost of your travels?

- What kinds of activities interest you in your travels?

Will you work?

- Would you like to continue working in retirement?

- Do you wish to begin a second career?

- What do you enjoy doing?

- Do you have any hobbies that you would like to try to turn into a source of income?

- Do you want to continue working in your present position, only cutting back on the amount of work you do?

- Do you want to volunteer your time to a public service organization?

Where will the money come from?

- Do you currently have any money saved for retirement?

- Are you willing to do whatever it takes to save the money necessary to achieve your early retirement goals?

The more thought-out your visions of the future become, the easier and more fulfilling it will be to plan for them. After all, it is more difficult to save when we do not know what we are saving for, but once we have a concrete goal in mind, saving to achieve that goal becomes a far less daunting task.

This book outlines an essential three-step plan for early retirement, but do not let that fool you into thinking that retiring early is going to be easy. Envisioning your future is only the first piece of the puzzle. You must continue to plan and prepare for your retirement as though it were going to begin tomorrow. Then, when the time comes you will be prepared.

Now, you have some clear indication of what your retirement will look like or what you want it to look like. Here are a few other things you need to think about.

WILL YOU HAVE A WORKING RETIREMENT?

It is very common for people to retire from their hectic, working-for-someone-else, 40-hour-per-week job only to find themselves bored and wanting to do something. While no one wants to remain at that dead end job the rest of their lives, most 50, 60, and even 70 year olds want and often should do something else. Is this you? Perhaps you have some of these goals in mind:

- Do you plan to work part time for your current employer? Perhaps you even want to work for a different employer? Consulting is a very large part of the business of retirees.

- Do you want to start a new career, one that you have put off all these years because you just have not had the time to do anything else? You may not even know what this career is just yet.

- Perhaps you want to become a business owner? Approximately a third of all those that retire early will become business owners on some level, whether it is a hobby style business, creating their own business just like that of their employer, or perhaps even just using their skills to freelance and consult.

- Do you want to further your education? For many, it means learning something new and even getting into more advanced levels of education.

- Is there something else you would like to do?

There is another side to this coin. For many people that do retire from their positions, there is a need to work at least part time. They may not have the options listed above, but they may need to work to make ends meet. Often this has to do with medical insurance. For others, it is a necessary tool to put food on the table and pay the never ending mortgage. If you work through the guidelines offered here, though, we will make sure that you are not one of the many that have found themselves in a position in which they have to work when they retire.

YOU WILL LIKELY LIVE LONGER

Another factor to take into consideration through all your retiring planning is that you will likely live longer than your parents or their parents did. With the advancements in medicine and the various ways that doctors can prolong life there is a likelihood that you will live several years longer. This is also due to the fact that people are taking better care of themselves. They are smoking less, drinking less, and eating healthier.

Financial planners will tell you that living to a ripe old age of 95 should be what you plan for. At least you or your spouse is likely to do so and therefore you should plan on this.

This book is not necessarily about planning just for those retirement years, though. We want you to be able to retire early, which means that you will need even more additional funds and planning. It is recommended that you do plan to work at least part time in your early retirement years. When you do this, you will be able to enjoy an early retirement with more time on your hands. You do not want to find yourself with plenty of time but with nothing to do.

WHAT IT MEANS TO RETIRE EARLY

With that idea in mind, consider what retiring early will mean for what you need to do right now. You need to plan for a retirement that suits your desires and needs. When you retire earlier than age 65, you will need to plan additional time into that retirement, which means having to plan for additional money.

What is early retirement anyway? While Baby Boomers are likely to believe that they will retire by the time they are 65 (62 for early retirement) younger generations do not have the same plans. Those that are in their late 20s to early 40s are planning on retiring before they hit 50 years of age. You can make this happen with a plan. About half of Generation X (those born between the years of 1964 to 1981) believes that retiring before 60 is a good goal, while the other half wants to retire a decade before.

The word retirement still has not been defined here. Of those that do want to retire early, only a small amount of them want to spend their days watching soap operas and talking to the neighbors about politics. Most will continue to stay busy during their "retirement" years.

WHEN DO YOU WANT TO RETIRE?

While there are government studies and reports showing that people are retiring earlier and earlier, that matters very little to you. It is up to you to determine when you really want to retire. You need to put a number to the term "early retirement." It will become an intricate part of your plan for success.

You may decide that you want to retire by the time you are 45. You should realize that there will be bumps in the road to getting there, no matter how well you plan. What is important to realize is that planning to retire means having a benchmark to base your goals on. Becoming ill or having to lose a job or two along the way may make 45 into 47 or 48, but that is still much closer than 65 will be.

While this book is all about the right methods to retiring early, do not be misled that it will be a piece of cake to make happen. The fact is that it will take a long time to complete the project, and it will be difficult for many people to make happen. Yet, with perseverance you can accomplish the goals that you set out to achieve, and you will be able to retire much earlier than you expect.

WHAT DOES RETIREMENT HOLD FOR YOU?

It is crucial for you to take something else into consideration as you plan for your retirement years. What will you do with all that time on your hands? What you do during retirement will define exactly what you need to plan for. If you plan to travel around the world every year, you must plan for that expense.

If you retire early, this means that you will have 30 to 50 years or more of your life ahead of you, with nothing to do. That is a long time and a lot of money needs to be accumulated to get to that point.

Here is a task that you must complete to really see where your money needs to go. Finish this sentence:

"When I retire, I want to ...."

You can list small things and big things. But fill that page with options and things that you want to do when you have the time. Here are some ideas to think about:

- Vacations and locations around the world that you want to visit

- New activities that you want to learn how to do

- Business goals that you may have

- Friendships that you want to make

- Daily activities that you want to be able to do

- Things that you know that you will need to do

- What your spouse wants to do

You will likely become bored if you have nothing to do. When you have options because you planned for them, there will be plenty of time and money to do all of those things that will keep you busy.

Did you know that two thirds of those that retire early go back to work and it is often because they are bored? While this is just fine, giving yourself the ability to do more by planning to do more may keep you out of the business of running around that much better.

HAVE YOU CONSIDERED WHAT YOU WILL LOSE?

Although most people know that when they retire they will be losing that boring old job, most do not realize that they are also giving up their salary. Perhaps you retire at the age of 50 with a paycheck that brings in $100,000 per year. Even so you still will not be receiving that paycheck any longer and that means a serious drop in your funds.

There is much more to retiring than just giving up the $100,000 paycheck. You are also losing out on bonuses and pay increases. You are losing out on all types of benefits. Even if you worked with a company that still offers a pension, this is minimized significantly in terms of how much money you are losing.

You also will be giving up your health care. This is one of the worst parts of retiring early because of how crucial it can be to every day life and how expensive it is to obtain on your own. Most people do not realize the cost of their insurance because they get it from their employer.

Health care becomes more important as you age, not less important. Therefore, you will need to overcome this situation in some form. There are options, including COBRA. COBRA is short for the Consolidated Omnibus Budget Reconciliation Act of 1985. This federal law requires that your employer allow you to maintain your enrollment in the group health plan for 18 months after you leave the company. To take advantage of this service, you have to pay 100 percent of the premium, as well as 2 percent of the paperwork costs. This still gives you a much lower cost than paying out of your own pocket because this is a group cost rather than an individual plan.

At the end of 18 months, you will need to find your own health insurance provision. This is something we will explore in a later chapter.

Another aspect that you are giving up by retiring, which you may not have thought about, is your social life, especially the relationships you have developed with your co-workers. You are losing some of that people contact, and you will have to replace this social interaction somehow.

What about your identity? For example, when you meet a new couple, you may introduce yourself in a specific way: "Hello, I'm James. I work at the newspaper down the street." Even if you do not use this in your introduction, people will ask you what you do for a living. What will you tell them? You may be able to tell them about the trips you and your spouse are taking around the world.

WHAT DID YOU LEARN?

With all this kept in mind, realize that you can invest

in the retirement you are envisioning. There are several things that you need to keep in mind:

1. You can retire at any age if you start making decisions today that will make it happen. Planning to retire at 40, 50, or even just to have a successful retirement at 65 can be done if you plan now.

2. What you plan to do in your retirement will determine how much money you need to have to retire.

3. Remember that retirement can mean starting a whole new life. You may work part time, start your own business, or travel the world.

4. Remember too that your grocery shopping will not be enough interaction to keep you happy all those years of retirement. You'll need more than that to be happy.

5. Making decisions today can help you create the type of retirement you did not think you could have. Start now while you have time, and you can create the life you are dreaming of, not settling for.

CHAPTER 2

YES, MONEY IS NECESSARY

Retirement will require many things, but perhaps the most important is having the perseverance to make it happen. It will take time to work through the process of creating the retirement that you want. There are sure to be problems and stumbling blocks along the way. You may even come to the decision that you want instant gratification rather than putting it off until retirement. Perhaps you want to stop for a second and contemplate exactly what retirement means to you. When you look at your paycheck, you see that there are deductions taken out. Social Security is deducted as a promise to give you back something when you do stop working. You have Medicare, which you are funding to help provide for your medical needs when you do retire. The problem, though, is that those funds are not enough. On top of that, as mentioned previously, it is now commonly thought that the Baby Boomer generation will wipe out Social Security for younger generations.

When you want to have a retirement that others will be envious of, you must have dedication to make it happen. Unfortunately, you also need money.

Money is a large factor in creating the type of retirement you are planning. Throughout this book we will show you how to create this type of money, but you have to be dedicated to making it happen. You will need to realize that there is no simple way to make it happen, but rather a sheer understanding that through determination you will make it happen.

The amount of money you will need for retirement is based on what you plan to do in retirement. You need to estimate what that amount will be. While it is easy living life when you have another paycheck coming in two weeks, retirement is much different, which often makes it harder to estimate your money needs.

WHERE WILL THE MONEY COME FROM?

Where will the money that you need to retire on come from? There are several factors you can control that will help you fund your retirement:

1. **Desire:** Desire to make it happen.

2. **Effective Decisions:** Provide the power for it to happen.

3. **Defense:** Against other situations.

4. **Discipline:** You have to have control.

When those four things, all of which you can control, are put in line, you can retire early and have your dream retirement.

Do not make the mistake of thinking that a get rich quick scheme will happen for you. Do not believe that somehow you will come into a huge amount of money. If these things do happen, take advantage of the additional wealth. Never stop planning for a life that does not have any type of windfall, though.

Now we will consider some of the other sources of money that you may be counting on to fund your retirement. This will help you clearly see what the future has in store for you.

ARE YOU COUNTING ON A PENSION?

Before you go any further, pick up the phone and call your employer's human resource director. Find out if you have a pension. Does your company even offer them? Many are forgoing the pension and providing those benefits in other ways to their employees. You may not have one.

There are a handful of opportunities out there, normally offered by the government or large corporations. Some will even offer an early pension to you. But do not assume that this is going to be a good idea.

The key problem with selecting a pension to fund

retirement is a failure to take into account the rate of inflation. Most pensions do not offer any benefit for this. For example, if the cost of living continues to rise every year at a rate of 4 percent, within the next 20 years you will have only half of the same money (in terms of value not number). While your pension numbers may sound good now, they are not likely to be good throughout your retirement.

Find out if your pension plan does take the rate of inflation into account. Make your decisions based on this information.

SOCIAL SECURITY WILL TAKE CARE OF YOU, RIGHT?

Social Security was put into place back in the 1930s. Today it is still a major source of income for those that do retire. The plan was simple then. Invest a small portion of your paycheck into Social Security, and when you hit age 65 you would have a check every month to help you to pay for what you need. The good news was that people did not have to continue to work until they were 70, 75, or older. They could retire and count on the income from Social Security to help pay for it.

The problem with this situation is that Social Security now has to fund the Baby Boomer generation, which will put an enormous strain on it. Some experts believe the system will fold, while others believe that it is only a matter of time before the system simply runs dry. In any of these situations, the problem is that Social Security may not be enough to get you through retirement.

There is still more to consider here. If you want to retire early, you are likely to face another problem. Social Security is pushing back the age at which you can retire. The reasoning behind this is as simple as the fact that people are living longer. While in 1930 you may have been considered very old at 70, now that number is 90 or older. This does not mean that you should not receive Social Security at 65 because you are not old enough, but because you are likely still able to work a full-time job at that age.

Therefore, if you want full benefits from Social Security, you will need to use this chart as a guideline as to when you can begin to claim it.

BIRTH YEAR	AGE FOR FULL BENEFITS
1938	65 and 2 months
1939	65 and 4 months
1940	65 and 6 months
1941	65 and 8 months
1942	65 and 10 months
1943-1954	66
1955	66 and 2 months
1956	66 and 4 months
1957	66 and 6 months
1958	66 and 8 months
1959	66 and 10 months
After	67

The goal of this was not only to help you work longer, but to keep the strain off the Social Security administration. In addition, the longer you hold out in getting Social Security, the more your benefits will increase. For example, between the ages of 66 and 70, you will see an increase of 6 percent in your benefits per year. There is no benefit increase after the age of 70, though.

That sounds great, right? Remember that this book is discussing how you can retire early. Waiting until you are at age 70 is not likely to be the best route to take to get to that point.

For those that do plan to use Social Security to aid their retirement plan, that is perfectly acceptable, but it should not be counted on. As the population ages, there will be an incredible amount of people entering retirement at one time. This Baby Boomer generation is the main problem, but it does not slow much after this. Not only will the government be strained in terms of providing you with Social Security, but virtually all aspects of government will feel the pressure to help the aging population.

HOW MUCH MONEY?

If we define financial freedom as having enough money to spend the rest of our time doing the things that we really want to do, we can understand why planning for that opportunity as early as possible is an important decision. Too often, when planning retirement — whether it is on time or early — people do not adequately determine how much money they are going to need. So, while no one ever plans on depleting their retirement savings, they often fail to plan far enough into the future.

You need to formulate a clear picture of exactly how

much money you need to save today so you have plenty of money for your future. Your retirement plan will certainly not be perfect, but using this book as a resource will help you begin making better decisions regarding your savings and investments.

In the end, simply working through the process of retirement planning, regardless of your current age, will increase the likelihood that you will be financially prepared when you do retire, and you will feel a greater peace of mind in knowing that your savings are on track.

Here we will look quickly at a few examples and methods that can help you see the role money plays in retirement. We will go through the details later. First, it is a must to give you an idea of what amount of money you will need.

Step One:

The first step to adequate financial planning is to determine how long your retirement will be. This is based on the questions that you answered in Chapter 1, regarding the age at which you wish to retire and your life expectancy. If you are feeling uncertain about your estimated life expectancy, it is best to err on the side of longevity rather than make a low estimate that will cause you to deplete your savings too early.

To determine the approximate length of your retirement, subtract the age at which you plan to retire from the age to which you expect to live. This will give you a better idea of how long of a retirement to plan for. Play around a bit with this. Perhaps retiring at 50 is ideal for you, giving you 40 years or more of retirement. You may want to retire earlier or later. For now, choose a number that can be used as your basis for the rest of this planning.

Step Two:

Next, you will need to determine your annual retirement expenses in today's market. To figure this out, consider both your current and future living expenses, as well as lifestyle expenses, such as travel, hobbies, and other recreational activities.

This is the hard part. But you can assume that you will at the very least maintain your current life style. In other words, the amount of money you need to live today is likely to be the same or more when inflation is taken into consideration.

You should consider your mortgage payment next. The reason for this is quite simple; you are likely to be paying a sizable amount of money for health insurance and that could be as large as your mortgage payment is today.

Your early retirement will likely encompass a 30- or 40-year span, so it is likely that your life style and expenses will change over that time. While you may travel less in late retirement, for instance, your health care expenses may significantly increase. Or you may finish paying for your home in mid-retirement or need to purchase a new car. It is helpful, then, to estimate your expenses during these three phases of your retirement. This will help you develop a clearer picture of your retirement expenses in the long-term.

When figuring out your expenses for retirement, be sure to consider the cost of those large, occasional items that you might purchase, such as a new car or a home renovation. If you add between two and five thousand dollars annually to your retirement expense total, this should help you be adequately prepared for such expenses.

Step Three:

Unfortunately, it is unlikely, if your retirement is still 15, 20, or 30 years away, that everything will cost the same as it does today. The process with which the cost of goods rises and the value of dollars falls is called inflation. When considering your future retirement expenses, it is important to adjust for inflation so that you do not grossly miscalculate the amount of money you will need to set aside to secure your future.

To do this, you will need to consider how far away your retirement goal is and what rate of inflation you can expect from the economy. This does not only mean that the cost of living will increase over time, but that costs will continue to increase throughout the course of your retirement. The table below will help you determine how much your costs will increase annually, depending on the rate of inflation.

RATE OF INFLATION PER # OF YEARS			
	3%	4%	5%	6%
1	1.03	1.04	1.05	1.06
2	1.06	1.08	1.10	1.12
3	1.09	1.12	1.16	1.19
4	1.13	1.17	1.22	1.26

RATE OF INFLATION PER # OF YEARS			
	3%	4%	5%	6%
5	1.16	1.22	1.28	1.34
6	1.19	1.27	1.34	1.42
7	1.23	1.32	1.41	1.50
8	1.27	1.37	1.48	1.59
9	1.30	1.42	1.55	1.69
10	1.34	1.48	1.63	1.79
11	1.38	1.54	1.71	1.90
12	1.43	1.60	1.80	2.01
13	1.47	1.67	1.89	2.13
14	1.51	1.73	1.98	2.26
15	1.56	1.80	2.08	2.40
20	1.81	2.19	2.65	3.21
25	2.09	2.67	3.39	4.29
30	2.43	3.24	4.32	5.74

The values in the table are found by using a simple financial formula for compound interest because inflation follows the same pattern as financial growth. These factors can also be found using a calculator with financial functions or by going through the retirement planning process with a well-trusted financial advisor.

To adjust your annual retirement expenses for future inflation, you will need to find your inflation factor, which is the number at the intersection between your rate of inflation and the row that represents your period of time.

Example 1:

If you are currently 40 and your goal is to retire at the age of 55, you have 15 years until retirement. To adjust for 5 percent inflation, you will look at the cell in the table where 5 percent and 15 years intersect. You will find the number 2.08. This is the number by which you will multiply your annual living expenses to determine your living expenses during retirement.

Remember, however, that inflation continues during retirement as well. Therefore, a well thought-out retirement plan will account for inflation that occurs while you are enjoying the life of a retiree. The easiest way to adjust for this is to consider the expected overall length of your retirement and adjust your expenses to the midpoint of your retirement. By using this method of calculation, your income target, adjusted for inflation, will be a rough average of the annual expenses over the course of retirement.

Example 2:

If you are 40 years old, plan to retire at the age of 55, and expect to live until the age of 85, the length of your retirement is 30 years. The midpoint of 30 is 15 years. So, when adjusting living expenses for inflation, it would be a good idea to add 15 years to the length of time until retirement, for a total of 30 years. At a 5 percent rate of inflation, they would multiply their living expenses by 4.32.

The next step to make an adjustment for inflation is to multiply the inflation factor that you find in the table by your determined annual expenses in today's dollars.

Example 3:

If you had determined that your living expenses during retirement would be an average of $20,000 per year in today's dollars, to adjust for inflation by the factor that we found in the previous example, you would multiply your living expenses by 4.32 (the inflation factor from that intersection of the table).

Step Four:

After you determine the annual income that you will need your investments to yield, you will need to determine the total nest egg that will yield that annual income. To determine this, you will need to know the amount of money you expect to withdraw during each year of retirement, as well as the expected length of your retirement and the rate of return that you expect on your investment.

Below is a table to help you determine the principal value factor for your investment, by which you will multiply your annual income to determine the lump sum that you will need for retirement. The figures in this table are derived from the financial formula for determining the present value factor. You can find them by using a calculator with financial functions or by speaking with your trusted financial advisor.

INTEREST EARNINGS RATE PER # OF YEARS TO WITHDRAW						
	5%	6%	7%	8%	9%	10%	15%
10	7.72	7.36	7.02	6.71	6.42	6.14	5.02
15	10.38	9.71	9.11	8.56	8.06	7.61	5.85
20	12.46	11.47	10.59	9.82	9.13	8.51	6.26
25	14.09	12.78	11.65	10.67	9.82	9.08	6.46
30	15.37	13.76	12.41	11.26	10.27	9.43	6.57
40	17.16	15.05	13.33	11.92	10.76	9.76	6.64

Example:

We have determined that your living expenses are $86,400 per year. Since you expect to live until the age of 85, you can expect to need this amount of money each year for 30 years. We need to determine the lump sum of money that would enable you to continue that income over the course of 30 years. If we expect a 9 percent return on the investment, to find the lump sum, we will multiply $86,400 by 10.27, the present value factor. The product is $887,328, the total amount of money that you would need to invest at a 9 percent rate of return to achieve the desired income of $86,400 each year for 30 years.

Do not be afraid of or disheartened by the lump sum that you find when completing your own calculations. Remember that this figure is adjusted for inflation over the years until the midpoint of your retirement. It overcompensates for your goal so that you are well prepared at the time of your retirement. This overcompensation will prove to be helpful when you take into account the taxes and penalties involved in withdrawing from your retirement funds early — a topic which we will discuss later in this book. Also, keep your other sources of income in mind: Early in your retirement, you may continue to work part-time, while later in retirement you may be entitled to fixed sources of income, such as pensions or Social Security, which will produce a small portion of your income.

In the end, what is most important in planning for your early retirement is being prepared. The significance of this lump sum is to provide a goal that will increase your odds of preparedness. The following steps will help you make the lump sum a little less intimidating and further help you itemize your exact needs for the future.

Step Five:

The next step in planning for your retirement is determining the current assets that you hold that will provide future retirement income. These assets can include savings, 401(k)s, personal retirement accounts, and anything else that you currently hold that will provide future retirement income. You will want to take the time to list out each of these aspects on a piece of paper so that you can see all the details.

You need this worksheet that will help you list these items and their current value, as well as look at how their value will appreciate over time. On the worksheet, you will list the assets that you are willing to sell or utilize to achieve your retirement goals, such as in the next example. Create your own version with as many assets as you feel necessary to reach your goal.

Example:

ASSET	CURRENT VALUE $	EXPECTED RATE OF RETURN %	POTENTIAL VALUE AT TIME OF RETIREMENT $
401(k)	$50,000	8%	$158,500
Real property	$150,000	6%	$360,000
Savings	$10,000	4%	$18,000
IRA	$15,000	9%	$54,600

In this example, you are still 40 years old and plan to retire at the age of 55. Here is the formula you need to figure out how much money you would have if you put n as the number of years until retirement.

$$A = P (1 + r)n$$

Where:

A is the amount of money accumulated after n amount of years, including interest

P is the principal (the initial amount you borrow or deposit)

r is the annual rate of interest (percentage)

n is the number of years the amount is deposited or borrowed for

In the example, the value of n when finding the compound interest factor is 15.

When you complete your own retirement plan, the potential value of your assets at the time of retirement is found by multiplying the compound interest factor for the number of years that you have until your retirement goal and the rate of return that you expect for that asset, by the principal value of that asset. You can use a calculator with financial functions or by speaking to a trusted financial advisor.

After finding the potential future value of all your assets, you will want to add those values together and subtract the total from the lump sum that you will need for your retirement.

In the example in the previous section, the total potential value of all the assets at the time of retirement is $591,100.

That is the amount that you can expect to already have saved at the time of retirement.

This total is then subtracted from the total lump sum that we determined you would need to produce $86,400 each year for 30 years during retirement.

This means $887,328 is the lump sum needed in the example. Take away the current value of assets, which is $591,100, and the end result is $296,228, which is the required capital that needs to be found to meet the goals of this particular retirement plan.

The difference between the total of your current assets and the total lump sum that you need to invest is your savings goal between now and the time that you plan to retire. In short, this is the answer to the question: How much do you need?

It is important to know that this lump sum is only an estimate, rather than an exact figure. What it is meant to do is to get you to set an attainable goal for which you can aim. While this goal may stretch you, as you will see later in this book, it is not intended to break you or deprive you of those things that are meant to make life enjoyable in the present.

Furthermore, there are a number of unplanned events that might come your way while you are attempting to save for early retirement — the best thing you can do to prepare for these events is to keep your savings plan intact. Deal with bumps in the road as they come along and continue contributing to your savings as before.

Now that you have found the lump sum that you will need to invest for your investment to last through retirement, the next logical step is to determine how you are going to get there. How much will you need to put away each month between now and the day you retire to achieve the lump sum that will repay you in the coming years?

This is what we will determine in the coming chapters — exactly how much money to put away every month and where to find the funds that you will need for your investments.

PLANNING FOR MORE

Here we focus on providing you with details and scenarios that could play out while you are planning for retirement.

For example, there are a number of things that could go wrong and likely will become a factor. While you can plan for these things, you do need to keep in mind that kinks can happen and likely will.

Here are some things to think about:

- What will happen if and when the stock market underperforms for a longer period than is considered "normal?"

- What will you do if Social Security payments are reduced?

- What if inflation skyrockets?

- What if an emergency happens that costs you much more than you thought it would?

- What if you or your spouse becomes ill, needs a nursing home, or long-term care?

There is little doubt that something will be lurking around the corner. One of the largest considerations when planning your retirement should be if you live longer than your money can take care of you for.

When situations like this arise, you should have a plan in place for them. First, determine now what you believe the best option would be.

Should you:

- Try to increase the amount of money that you have going into retirement to provide for those "what if" situations?

- Plan to reduce your cost of living and retirement goals to cut back on what you will need during this time?

- Hope for the best?

Of course you want to provide yourself with a cushion because a cushion helps to keep you living the life you want. What is more, scaling back on your standard of living is not likely to help simply because many people will face these large problems well beyond the time when they can make changes. For example, if you hit age 80 and need long-term care facilities, you will have likely used your retirement money up until that point to provide the standard of living that you want, and you will not have the ability to cut back enough to afford this situation.

The bottom line is that you need to set your own goals for financial freedom during your retirement years, and when you have them in place, put in action the steps to make them happen.

WHAT ELSE GOES INTO YOUR RETIREMENT PLAN?

While money is the foundation of any successful retirement plan, it is not, by any means, the only consideration that you should have. In fact, you will need to take into consideration more of what goes into the recipe for success here, starting with your ability to stick with the course.

Here are several additional tools that you must take into consideration if you are to be successful in your retirement plans.

Desire: How Badly Do You Want It?

Desire is perhaps something that will change over the course of your retirement planning. You may want it more now than later. You need to consider how badly you want to have a successful retirement and what you are willing to do now to obtain it.

If you have the right level of desire, you can power through even the most difficult of times to obtain your goal.

In other words, you need to not only want to enjoy the benefits of retirement, but you must also see yourself doing it. You have to dream about it, envision it, and want it.

Having this amount of desire will help you get through all the obstacles along the way. Realize that the desire it takes will eventually help you accomplish your goals now and in the future. The satisfaction of knowing that you are planning a retirement that will be rewarding for you, your spouse, and perhaps your children may be a reward in itself.

Perhaps this is not something that you can do right now. You may not have the desire that it takes. That is quite understandable. No matter what you feel about this, using the information here can help you enjoy a truly amazing journey and even help you prepare for retirement later rather than earlier. The goal right now, then, is to determine if you have the desire to work hard to achieve this goal.

Hard Effective Decisions: Every Decision Will Matter

In the grand scheme of things, one small decision here or there may not seem like a big deal. Yet the combined effort of all your decisions determines the success of your retirement plan. When you can put together the pieces of a successful goal, you will put yourself in the position of achievement.

Every choice you make from today forward affects the results of your retirement plan. Some will not affect reaching your goal; others will. The thing that you must learn is which decisions will affect the long-term goals that you make.

For example, it may not be the first decision that causes the problem, but secondary financial consequences that come from that first decision may hurt you. When you do have important choices like this, take the time to think them through and analyze all aspects of the positive and negative.

What type of decisions may these be? They may be decisions such as:

- Getting married

- Getting divorced

- Funding your child's college education

- Helping your parents

- Vacations that you take

- Having another child

Or there could be those that are related to your employment. This can include things like:

- Leaving your position for a new one

- Quitting your job

- Starting your own business

- Transferring to another location

- Furthering your education

The little decisions also make a difference. For example, many people do not realize that those small purchases can add up. If you are someone that eats out just two times per week, you may see this as a luxury that you allow yourself or even something you do because you do not have time for dinner. Chances are good, however, that you are spending too much.

For a family of four, this is likely to be about $40 per time out or $80 per week, $320 per month, or $4,160 per year. Since you often can make the same food at home for about 25 percent of the cost, this means that you are overspending by $3,120 per year by eating out. Now, flip this around and see this as a plus. If you stay in just half of that time, you can easily save yourself $1,500 a year. That money can then be put into savings or into your retirement plan to help you to achieve your goal that much faster.

Compound that with interest, and you could easily save thousands of dollars for your retirement. At 8 percent compounded interest, that $1,500 a year could help you save nearly $120,000 dollars in just 25 years. That is a serious consideration for anyone looking for a way to add to their retirement plan. Of course, you should look at other monthly expenses to see if this $125 per month could actually be more.

Here is the bottom line: To have later in life, you have

to make some decisions that will limit what you can have today. The question is: Can you provide yourself with satisfaction in meeting your goals today and make decisions that will allow you long-term results as well?

The best resource to helping you to create this incredible opportunity is called compound interest. In a basic definition, it is interest paid to the account, and then that new sum has interested applied to it. This means that the first month your deposit would look small and the interest not much, but because it compounds, the interest builds faster the larger the account is and the longer it is in place.

Now, do not make the mistake of believing that you have to live a life of frugality to obtain your retirement goals. That is not the case. You have to make decisions that may limit you somewhat to get the end result. As in the example earlier, you do not have to take away every night that you eat out each week, but limiting it to just one night can help you save thousands of dollars. You still get some of the luxury, but you put some of that luxury away for later, too.

When you can do this, you can make a considerable amount of money for your retirement.

Discipline: Putting It in Motion

Stop for a moment and think about something. Think of all the things you "have to do." How many of them are things that you have been putting off? The more you put off, the longer it takes to accomplish those goals.

The same is true of retirement planning. Delaying cuts time off the compounding interest you are looking for. The longer it takes you to get the ball rolling, the longer it will take to build up the money you will need or the more you will need to invest.

While you do not have to sit down today and work out the entire plan, put it into motion tomorrow and work on it every day thereafter. You do need to make a commitment to put together a successful plan and keep it going in the right direction.

You will need to sacrifice the small things from time to time to reach the larger goals. Remember these two rules:

1. Do not put off what you can do today.

2. Do not deny yourself, but do not pamper yourself beyond what hinders your retirement dreams and goals.

DEFEND YOUR FUTURE

You have thought about what you want from retirement; now put the wheels in motion. There will be risks. But, if you can somehow work into your plan the right risks and make decisions accordingly, you may be able to forgo some of the worries and painful situations that could hurt you in the long run.

Making the right decisions is an important part of being successful. Yet recognizing those situations that pose a larger threat can help you avoid the pitfalls. It is much easier for you to keep up your goals, but when you fall behind it can be difficult to pull yourself up either monetarily or emotionally.

Therefore, avoid risks that are too high and that could put your retirement in jeopardy.

From this section, you can see how important it is to be disciplined in managing your life style now so that later you will have what you need to enjoy retirement. Do not believe that you must give up everything. Instead, realize that by putting a bit of effort into the plan now, you can have what you want now and later.

CASE STUDY: MARTIN E. KNIGHT

A question often asked is this. Everyone is different with their goals and expectations for retirement. How can a person prepare for what they want if they do not know what they want? The answer is fairly straightforward. It is all about options — if retirement goals and expectations are unclear, planning must leave as many options open as possible.

Once the person is through the accumulation/saving phase of their life it is almost impossible to repair a lack of funding for the "ideal" retirement — whatever that is determined to be.

Many people believe that they can do the financial planning for retirement on their own. Simply putting away enough money seems like a good enough solution. But investing in a professional is a key element to being successful.

CASE STUDY: MARTIN E. KNIGHT

People can do it on their own — but it can be very costly. I can change the oil in my car, too — but again, it can be very costly if I forget to put the oil filter on properly. A number of studies have shown that the average investor does not come close to what the market returns — due to personal emotions and public business cycles, most people end up buying high and selling low.

An advisor can help clients through the variety of market conditions — often by simply explaining the long-term behavior of stock markets and the distinct ability of the "experts" in the media to get it wrong.

Anyone can retire — but living comfortably in retirement takes work. The streets of any major city have scores of people who have retired without putting forth effort, with little to no planning — but they are not very comfortable living on the steam grate for heat in the winter.

People must prepare for the time when they either no longer want to work for a wage; are unable physically to work for a wage; or offer no value to an employer to hire them. At that point — be it called retirement or just unemployment — they must use their own funds to maintain a comfortable lifestyle.

Martin E. Knight, MBA
President, Chesapeake Investment Advisors, Inc.
800-994-0221
mknight@chesadvisors.com

Centreville Office
203 N. Commerce Street
Centreville, MD 21617
Office: 410-758-4648
Toll Free: 800-994-0221
Fax: 410-758-9842

Chestertown Office
106 Spring Ave.
P.O. Box 480
Chestertown, MD 21620
Office: 410-810-0735
Fax: 410-810-3422

Securities and Advisory Services offered through Geneos Wealth Management, Inc. Member NASD/SIPC

3 IT IS NOT A SIMPLE CUT AND DRY DEAL

During retirement, you could spend your days doing anything you wanted and simply enjoy life. Life rarely is that easy to manage, though. When you want to have a retirement that others will be envious of, you must have dedication to make it happen. Unfortunately, you also need money.

The problem is that retirement is a new life style that takes getting used to and it causes you to take on a new emotional role for you. For many, nothing can keep them from sitting back and relaxing or enjoying a game of golf every few days. For others, having something meaningful to do is the key to being happy.

In terms of life style changes, two types are found. First, your financial world changes; you no longer have that income coming in, and your spending is completely different. The second change is emotional. The world is different through the eyes of someone in retirement and rightly so. You must prepare yourself for all types of situations so that you are better prepared for success in any case.

Retiring early will mean the onset of even more situations.

GIVING UP WHO YOU ARE

Perhaps the largest problem with retiring is giving up who you are. As defined by your employment, you are someone. You may be a manager or you may be in the business of helping others. The fact remains that you are someone and you have specific duties. You do not have to hold an important position to feel this way either. Your self-esteem knows that you are important to someone, something, or for something.

When you retire, you lose that good feeling because you are no longer contributing in the same way to your business, employees, customers, or even just society. That is a blow to anyone's self-esteem. The fact that the world can go on without you doing what you do great can really hurt.

The best way to get around this feeling is to have something to do. Why would this be mentioned here? While this book is not about helping you find something to do, it does require a close look at what you will do so that can be planned for.

Take, for example, the story of Lisa and Ken. They planned to retire when they were just 50 years old. They invested and did well. Ken retired first, but did it in a unique way. Instead of just leaving his job outright one day, he decided to slowly pull away.

To do this, he started to take Fridays off. He kept working Monday through Thursday, but took the long weekend. He and Lisa quickly found things to do that they enjoyed, and those long weekends were nice. Next, he stopped working Mondays, and that too increased the time he could spend with his new hobbies. He enjoyed small trips and getting to spend more time helping his children with their homes.

But when it was Lisa's turn to begin to pull out of her job, she wanted more. She was a school teacher and loved the thrill and excitement of having a new set of students each year. Most important, it was not going to be possible for her to slowly cut back. She needed something else. She did not feel that she wanted to leave behind the children, though. Although Ken and Lisa were financially ready to retire, Lisa was not ready for the emotional separation.

For Ken, it was easy to find things to do and to slowly pull out of his business. This was not possible for Lisa. Therefore, the plan for them was to find something new to concentrate on and hopefully that would give Lisa that emotionally beneficial result she was after.

Lisa and Ken did find this. Lisa found that becoming a foster parent was an ideal choice for them since they had a large home and a lot of love. Her education and experience with children helped to give them the drive they needed. Within a year, they both were able to stay home. Ken still consulted at his business because he wanted something professional to do, although this amounted to just a handful of hours per week. Lisa did great helping children, and they soon took in two young boys.

The moral of this story is that you must find a way to not only build a financial net for yourself through retirement, but also to have the emotional support that you need. What is more, if it is possible to slowly withdraw from your place of employment like Ken did, you may find yourself less strained.

From a financial point of view, you will be able to see that you may need to make adjustments to your retirement plan to accommodate these goals. For Ken and Lisa, they did not need to invest much more with their plan for becoming foster parents mainly because they had most of what they needed. But with more mouths to feed, clothing to purchase, and toys and outings to pay for, they did need to increase their yearly capital.

Lucky for them, Ken continues to consult several years after he planned to retire, which gives them some additional money. Moreover, Lisa offers some help to the school system. She works as a tutor because she loves to teach, and the family is supplemented by the government for taking on two children. They are well ahead of where they need to be in terms of financial security.

Look at your own goals. If you were to take on something to "do" during your retirement years, would you have the funds put aside to accomplish that goal?

After you have taken a hard look at the financial needs that your emotional dependence on activity and social reaction requires, you can move into the planning stages of your retirement income. A word of caution: You simply must not assume that you will be fine without any activity.

UT IT IS RETIREMENT! WHY SHOULD I WORK?

has been argued that the key to a long and happy life is find work that connects you to others, challenges you on any levels, and makes a difference in the world. So it is sy to see why finding work that you enjoy is important, en in early retirement. If you are one of the lucky ones no does not need the income, it is still important that u find a valuable way to spend your time. Paid or paid, you will need to find some way to stay engaged d challenged, or your early retirement years are likely quickly become unpleasant and surprisingly awkward. ing time, relaxing, and being self-indulgent are all nderful in small doses and surely seem appealing as ns of recuperation after years of overworking yourself. self-indulgences alone will not help you achieve your goal: to live a long, happy, and fulfilling life.

he beginning of your retirement, just keeping up the housework may seem like more than enough onsibility. Keeping your cars maintained and tered, the plumbing leaks fixed, and your gutters of leaves may be enough to keep you exhausted. But tually, you will want to take on more of a challenge.

truly happy, you will need to find something that es and challenges you. A well-chosen avocation in retirement can not only provide needed supplemental e, but actually support and even enhance the es you are making in your life. In addition to making appier and more fulfilled, scientists now argue that g the brain engaged wards off Alzheimer's disease, ental health professionals maintain that those who

Everyone goes through some level of withdrawal at the time of retirement.

GETTING PROFESSIONAL HELP

One aspect that has not been mentioned but that you absolutely should consider doing is getting help from a financial planner or a professional that can guide you through the process of investing and developing your money for retirement. A financial planner has the job of providing you with information and resources to help you make wise decisions for all your investment goals.

Many people wonder if they should pump their hard-earned money into someone that is simply going to manage it for them. After all, you can do the same thing, right? This is perhaps one of the biggest reasons people make the mistake of not hiring a professional. Financial advisors can help you make wise decisions about where to spend your money and where to earn the most for your particular goals.

A good planner is something that you must have by your side throughout the process. In a later chapter we will provide much more information about choosing and using a financial planner. Realize that the small investment that you make in one can help transform the success of your retirement plan, as well as any other need that arises along the way.

PLANNING THE FIRST YEARS

The first years of retirement can be the most difficult for those that have enjoyed working. You may want to retire and stop working day in and day out, but you may also realize that having something to do is important.

Here are several things that you need to focus on:

1. Take the time now to talk to your partner about retirement. What are your goals and dreams here and what are theirs? What do they see doing these years of their life and when do they want it to happen?

2. Plan activities, trips, and things to do for the first few years. As Ken and Lisa did, plan to have some type of meaningful activity for the first years of retirement so that you can be busy and not dreading every day.

3. Get something to do that is all about you. While you will spend much of your retirement with your spouse, you also need to have things to do on your own. Whether this is a sport, a club, or even a new business, find a way to have something that is all you.

4. Meet with a financial planner to talk about where you are right now. Find out what you need to do to get to the next point.

5. Keep reading. This will help you stay up to date on what is happening and help you improve your retirement plan. Come back to the plan often to find ways to tweak it. Even after you retire, you need to

focus on the financial and emotional aspects retirement.

WHAT IS REALLY THE POINT?

The point of early retirement is to free up your life to fulfill pursuits that are more meaningful to does not include doing nothing at all; you will as though you are wasting your time and begin where all the time has gone. By participating that keep your brain fresh, activities in wl count on you, or activities that help you devel unique skills, you can avoid falling into a de and develop a sense of extended efficacy.

If you are thinking about retiring early but taken the plunge, you may already have some you want to do in retirement. Perhaps you time for a former employer or backpack acr become a missionary in a small, African cou even plan to take classes or even earn a recast yourself into a new avocation. Or yo more than a vague hope that there will be s world that strikes your fancy.

Whatever you decide to do in retirement, it i you do something. If you choose to work to strike a balance between your work Hopefully, throughout the course of this develop a better idea of how to do just th

cut themselves off from meaningful interaction with others are more prone to depression after they retire.

THE EVOLUTION OF WORK: THREE STAGES

Work in early retirement will not look the same as it did earlier in your life. You will not want to recreate the same hyper-ambitious overachievement on a lower pay scale; you have chosen to retire early to make time and opportunities for a more comfortably-paced schedule.

Many early retirees start off by feeling that they could never adapt to a slower life style, but this — while a powerful and valid sentiment — reflects thinking anchored in the past. If you are able to find work activities that you feel are genuinely better and more fun than those you have been doing in your career, it will become much easier to make any necessary financial trade-offs to stay engaged in them. For instance, a former hard-nosed professional, after discovering her inner artist, might prefer to move to an inexpensive rural home, rather than go back to work to pay the taxes on an expensive home in the suburbs.

Early retirees normally go through many changes as they seek to find the right blend of paid and unpaid work activities and striking a balance based on need, appetite for challenge, and opportunity.

1. Most Money in the Least Time

Most early semi-retirees attempt to find work that will pay them the greatest amount of money for the least amount of time on the job. They want time for leisure after years of overworking themselves and look at work in the utilitarian terms of effort and reward.

If you are going through this stage, staying close to former employers where your network and skills are still strong will likely deliver the biggest payback and most opportunity for cutting back to a limited number of hours of work. Working limited hours each week can be an extremely liberating feeling while your early pension or safe withdrawal amount covers your expenses. You can find the joy in life again by spending your free time exploring and relaxing.

2. Cutting the Apron Strings

During this stage, the effects of all the time you have spent relaxing and thinking during early retirement will begin to show. This is when many retirees begin to drift away from their former careers, finding it uninteresting and often even toxic.

If your work begins to seem out of step with who you are as a person, you may find yourself in this stage. It may seem that you are becoming steeped in new possibilities, and you may be drawn to new ways of making money. Chances are, you would prefer to find something as pleasant as possible — and perhaps something that will require a drastic shift in gears. Now, you might not mind working more and earning less, if you can find work that you enjoy. In your free time, you might want to dig more deeply into some of your personal interests. Try taking classes, earning certificates, or otherwise preparing yourself for a new line of work. You are beginning to want to do what you love, rather than be forced to love what you do.

3. Being Paid for Doing What You Love

Those who develop their skills and become proficient in things that they care about often come to trust that there may be a way to earn income through them and gradually switch to seeking ways to get paid for doing what they love.

In this stage, you may notice that your relationship to money begins to change. Perhaps your portfolio has grown throughout the beginning of your retirement, offering you a bit of breathing room. Even if you are not feeling rich, you may find your way into a comfortable balance in which your income is actually covering all your expenditures. And you may begin to spend your days doing activities that are actually meaningful to you.

You have also likely spent much of your free time up until this point taking classes and building contacts in your area of interest, so that now you have the skills, contacts, credibility, and experience to work in an area that you love. With any luck, you will eventually be able to find additional income-generating possibilities in your emerging areas of interest. But, at this point, income will no longer be the defining driver of your decisions. Now, you would rather do something that you care about and live within the income that you can comfortably earn from it.

JUST DO IT: MAKE THE CHANGES

You may have been able to seek out a living during the first half of early retirement. Perhaps with an early pension, a safe withdrawal from your portfolio, and a little bit of income from work, you have been able to balance the numbers and come out with your income covering your expenses in the end. Or perhaps you started early retirement pleasantly and soon found that your optimistic miscalculations now make it necessary for you to earn a bit of income to supplement each year. Or perhaps you do not even need the income, but you have become bored with days filled with golf and surfing the Internet. Any way you look at it, finding work that is satisfying and enjoyable needs to become a priority.

BE PATIENT

First, you must understand that many people go through their entire lives without ever finding their true calling. That said, it is likely that even if you do find satisfying work, you will continue to collect an assortment of skills, interests, commitments, and sources of income, continuing to change your avocation throughout the years.

Keeping a sense of exploration and evolution will make it much more possible for you to enjoy this search for satisfaction than if you try to have everything set in stone.

Though you might long for a particular career change for a while, you do not simply wake up one morning and become a teacher or an artist. These things take training, determination, and time — which luckily you have plenty of at this point.

HOW MUCH?

There are two basic schools of thought regarding finding satisfying work in early retirement. By picking the one that fits you and your personality, you can create the path to your own happiness in retirement.

LIMITED WORK HOURS IN YOUR CURRENT CAREER

In this approach, you focus on the hours that you feel comfortable working, the level of demands that you could comfortably take on, and the amount of flexibility in your schedule that you need to keep from feeling imprisoned by your work commitments. This approach is normal among new early retirees who choose to stay near their former profession and networks. Consider building a blend of activities that provide the right amounts of work time, commitment, and expected income, while also offering variety and a chance to explore new opportunities.

FIND NEW INTERESTS

The second approach to finding meaningful work is best suited to those who are ready for bigger changes. Try thinking about what you really care about doing, regardless of financial rewards. Doing so will get you focused on new fields and new interests, and will give you a chance to create newfound passion and energy. This may come naturally as a second stage in the evolution of your work during early retirement. Or you may be ready to skip straight to it when first leaving your full-time job.

TAKE A BREAK

If you are leaving your old job feeling frazzled and burnt out, you might consider making a clean break and taking some time for yourself. Take a few months of unstructured and uncommitted time to clear your head and to do those things that you have always wanted to do.

That time will allow you the opportunity to refresh yourself, so that you can begin to clearly understand your own needs, interests, and goals. Give yourself that initial break that you have worked so hard to achieve. This time is about getting to know who you are in this new skin, so feel free to travel or to stay home, to become a hermit and finish the rest of the books on your reading list or to connect with old friends.

TAKE IT SLOW

Regardless of how much time you take off from work, it is highly unlikely that you will forget how to work. Feel free to take some time off from work without worrying, and do not begin to worry about work again until you reach your own comfortable footing.

4

LIFE CHANGES IN RETIREMENT AND BEFORE

As you age and your life begins to change, your dreams, plans, and goals may need to be amended to fit with your life style changes. Here we will discuss how these changes might affect your life after retirement and determine the steps that you can take to ease the transitional periods you might face.

Early in retirement many people enjoy an active life. But, after a period of time, life may change a bit. Travel becomes less extensive while activities become slower and closer to home. Still later, the activities may become less frequent and help may become more necessary. The age at which people move from one stage to is the next differs.

Issues like your health, changing housing needs, divorce, remarriage, death of a spouse, and needs of adult children, grandchildren, or aging parents may cause you to rethink your retirement dreams.

These or other possible changes in life are the reasons to have an emergency fund of three to six months of living expenses no matter what your age. When changes occur in life, whether large or small, having a written list of your goals will help direct your thoughts, as decisions regarding your life style changes must be made. When making these decisions, take your time, visit with those close to you, and consider the pros and cons of each possible choice.

ILLNESS AND HEALTH

Illness can affect your retirement life style and budget. Even with Medicare and a good supplemental insurance policy, you still may need to include expenses for prescriptions, home health services, and nursing home expenses in your budget. While you are still healthy, you can investigate several health care options. While making plans for potential illness in advance may not be a fun way to spend an afternoon, it can save you and your family a lot of headaches down the road.

The rates of coverage differ from one location to the next in terms of health insurance. And, by far, health insurance will be the largest cost for most people. As you need it more, the cost of health insurance rises. You can begin to understand why this is important to research now. That way, you can plan for this increased cost.

Here is the first problem. Currently, you cannot get Medicaid until you hit the age of 65, but if you want to retire at age 50, what will you do? That is why you need to know what your options are and how you will afford them.

One option that you will have is a non-group health care policy that comes from the company that ran your employer's health care coverage. A basic plan from this type of company can cost from $200 to $500 per month per person in the age range of 48 to 55. But that does not mean that those costs will continue on the same path.

For example, if the current cost of your health insurance is $6,000 per couple over the course of a year, in ten years, it will cost you $11,800. In 20 years, it will cost you, $23,200. And in 30 years time, that same insurance coverage will cost you $45,700. These factors take into consideration a 7 percent rate of inflation. If it will cost you more than this per year, take that additional cost into consideration.

Do not assume that when you hit 65 all will be well, though. The truth behind Medicare is that it was only put in place to provide for basic health care, not long-term, high quality care. Most often, it does not cover more than what is required during a hospital stay. Part B, which is an elective element of health care, is then withdrawn from your Social Security check every month, cutting into the amount of money you take home.

You may also want to consider investing in Medigap insurance, which helps to provide for additional health care coverage where Medicare leaves you out. This will be costly in many cases (there is a range of different options for Medigap, with the best being the most costly). This means that you need to find and invest in health care that will give you quality health coverage all your life without depending on what the government programs will offer you. Most important, this cost must be figured into your early retirement plan if you are to take advantage of what it can offer you.

HOUSING

When some people retire, they decide that their attachment to the memories in their home far outweigh any benefits that might be conceived in moving to a new location. For others, retirement is truly all about leaving their lifetime dwelling for a more comfortable place where the amenities of retired life are abundant.

When you retire, you will need to decide what the most important factor in your retirement dwelling is, and these needs may change over time. You may start out in your own home, but decide in later retirement that a simpler retired life in an assisted-living community works best for you.

What kinds of amenities are important to you? Do you want building security, grounds and building maintenance, or services such as meals, recreation, transportation, and laundry? As your housing needs change, you may want to consider universal design changes that allow you to remain longer in your current home comfortably or possibly look at housing options available in your community and a community to which you may move in the future.

Ninety percent of those that retire will stay in the area in which they are already living. Many times they stay in the same home, too. You may have already decided that you will be living some place else. In either instance, your goal here is to find the perfect place for your retirement years, but you have to plan for that.

For planning purposes, look closely at the process, costs, and situation of purchasing a home in the area in which you will likely live. You are not looking for that perfect home yet, but you should have some idea of the cost that it will take to get you to that point.

Here are some things to take into consideration:

1. Income taxes

2. Real estate taxes

3. Sales taxes

4. Property value

5. Purchases of late

6. Capital gains (they will get your money in some form)

7. Interest and dividend requirements

8. Pensions

9. Social Security

10. Retirement plans

When you take the time to learn about these costs now, you are better able to understand what it will take to move, or if moving is worth the cost. To get this information, contact the local city hall or the state department of revenue where you would like to move. In some areas, you will see an increase in the cost of living there. Multiply that by the overall length of your retirement and you may need much more money than you realized.

DIVORCE

When family assets are divided due to a divorce settlement, you must redraw your retirement picture. Throughout the retirement planning process, you have considered the needs and desires of your spouse along with your own, but as a single person you have an opportunity to create a new retirement picture.

Spend some time considering what you would like to do. As a newly-single individual, you can put your own wants and needs above any compromises that you may have made for your spouse, and the options that are open to you are virtually limitless. Start by adding up what you own and owe. Subtract what you owe from what you own to find your net worth. Then, you can begin making the decisions that will determine who and where you are in your retirement years.

DEATH OF A SPOUSE

Like divorce, the death of a spouse can potentially change your plans and goals for retirement a great deal. Plan ahead for this situation to save yourself grief and headaches if it occurs later in life.

may want to apply for a spousal benefit on their record if it would be larger than your widow's benefit. You cannot get both. If you have questions regarding the Social Security benefits of deceased spouses, you will want to contact your local Social Security office to learn how current rules might affect you.

If you are receiving company retirement benefits or an annuity from a deceased spouse's employment, find out how remarriage will affect that income before you remarry. Sometimes benefits end when you remarry. Other policies may remain in effect.

FAMILY CHANGES

Changes in the lives of family members may also alter your retirement picture. Your children may go through such events as divorce, death of a spouse, job loss, or loss of housing, and this can have a huge impact on your retirement plans.

While care of grandchildren may be an exciting benefit of retirement, it can also prove to be a limitation to enjoying your newly-found freedom. Often, grandparents might find themselves asked to care for children too frequently. It is up to you to decide how often, when, and where you are willing to care for grandchildren. Then make your wishes known.

Your life will continue to change in your retirement years, and as it does you may need to adjust your retirement goals and plans. What was important to you when you

You can begin by determining how much income you will have if you become a widow or widower. How much will it cost you to live? Some expenses will go down, but others may remain about the same.

When a spouse dies, you will need access to ready cash. You should plan to have enough money to pay for your spouse's final expenses and to pay for daily living for about six months. This money must be either in your name or in a joint account with rights of survivorship prior to the death. If accounts are in your spouse's name alone or titled in some other way, you may not be able to open the funds without a court order, which can require a lot of time and hassle.

To settle your spouse's estate, you will also need family, legal, financial, and debt records, so it can be helpful to ensure that your name is on the safe deposit box and that you have access to all other documents that you and your family may need. Time you spend gathering the information that you need early on will serve you well down the road.

If you will receive a lump sum of money from your spouse's employer, an annuity, inheritance, or other source, consider consulting a financial adviser for investment advice. Some financial advisers work on commission and others work on a fee-only basis.

Sometimes a widow or widower feels panic when decisions must be made, whether it is to sell the house, furniture, personal items, or invest a lump sum payment from life insurance. Many times several weeks or months pass until, suddenly, the person feels a strong need to decide.

In what appears to be a few minutes, the person makes a decision, often with little or no comparison shopping or input from advisers or family members. If you plan early, you can avoid allowing yourself to be sold into products you do not need, or forced into situations in which you have very few options.

Upon the death of your spouse, you should wait six months to make major decisions. By doing this, you allow yourself time to develop a more normal routine. During that time you can educate yourself about finances or other related topics before you reach a decision.

REMARRIAGE

Remarriage can be exciting, but it also presents some challenges and more decisions to make.

If you or your spouse have children from previous marriages, for instance, or if either of you have assets that you want to protect in case of divorce, you may want to prepare a prenuptial agreement. Financial advisers can assist you in planning a prenuptial agreement, but you will need to contact your attorney to discuss how a prenuptial might work for you and arrange to have one prepared.

Remarriage can also affect the Social Security status of a woman whose previous husband is deceased or vice-versa. If you remarry, you will continue to receive benefits on your deceased spouse's Social Security record. However, if your current spouse is a Social Security beneficiary, you began planning for your early retirement may become less important to you as you age. Establish relationships with trusted financial and legal advisers now so that you are prepared when these changes occur.

LEAVING SOMETHING BEHIND?

People have mixed feelings on this subject, but it must be said. Do you want to leave something behind to your children or heirs or do you want to use up every penny of what you have and forget about what happens after you are gone?

The problem with this type of situation is quite simply that you do not known when you will die. Some will die much earlier than others. What you need to consider is what your overall goals are in terms of using what you have during retirement.

As far as how long to plan on living, the best recommendation that can be given is to plan to live to age 95. The worst case scenario is that you run out of money before you run out of time. That means that you will struggle financially for the last years of your life, and this means sacrificing things like health care when it is most important to you. If you do die before you use up all the money you have, you will have an estate plan in place to help your family use what you have left.

Plus, if you hit age 90 and have too much money left, you will be able to use it more freely. Who does not want to go on a shopping spree at that age or take a trip around the world? But, if you run out too soon, you will not have money to pay for the most important things in life, and that is far too risky to consider.

CARING FOR YOUR PARENTS

Perhaps something that you did not think of is the fact that you may one day have to help take care of your aging parents. Imagine the face your father will make when you tell him, at the age of 50, that you are planning to retire. He, at the age of 75, may be quite impressed with your ability to do so, but realizes that he may need some help. Can he ask you for help in paying for his rising costs at this time in his life or will he feel that this would ruin your retirement?

If and when you consider the age of your parents or other people in your life, realize that you may want to help them financially later on. That means putting aside even more money. This is a large financial burden, and many people do not realize or plan for this. However, when choosing between caring for family and retiring early, most people will choose family.

To tackle this topic, make it a point of sitting down and talking to your spouse, who will play a role in what your goals are in this field. Your spouse's parents may also need the same type of back up plan. Next, plan a meeting with your parents to talk to them about their financial situation. Are they going to have enough to help them through all the "what if" situations? After reading this book, you will have a good idea of what they will need and may even be able to help them plan for their financial success.

Many parents will not be comfortable sharing this information with their children. If for no other reason than to not be embarrassed, they will simply shove it to the side or tell you not to worry about it. Make up your mind to help or not to help and then plan for that decision.

Perhaps your parents have plenty of money. If they allow you to, help them plan for the successful use of this money, as well as planning out their later years financially. This gives them the help they may need and helps you know they are set.

It is also very important to consider your parent's financial state in terms of your own. Many people make the mistake of planning their retirement based in part on what their families will leave to them through an inheritance. This is a huge mistake potentially because there is no real way of knowing if you are going to get something, how much taxes will be lost in the process, and how long they will live. Many times, parents do things that do not make sense, such as giving a larger portion of their estate to someone else or even spending every penny of it before they are gone. In any case, there are too many risks involved in incorporating your potential inheritance (which can also change at any time they are alive) into your retirement plan.

COLLEGE, CHILDREN, AND MONEY

As you age, you may have another child. You may very well wind up retiring and still having a child under the age of 18 to care for. You will need to have the financial means of providing for them.

Another consideration is college. Many people find that they do want to help their children and grandchildren with this expense. This is something else to think about as you plan for your early retirement.

Even if you have fully grown children, you probably would do just about anything to help them. What happens when they need to borrow money?

WHERE DO YOU STAND?

There is no way for you to plan for every situation like this, but having a rough idea of what could happen down the road will eventually help you pull things together for a retirement plan.

SO, WHAT DOES THIS MEAN TO YOU?

Take a good look at all that could happen and what that means to your retirement plan. While planning for your retirement may seem like a battle to accumulate all you can, it is not. What you do need to realize is that you need to make sure you are planning for as much as possible because life changes.

CHAPTER

5

HAVING MONEY AND BEING WEALTHY

eing wealthy sounds like a great goal, but do you realize that wealth has much less to do with how much money you have and how much money you spend? It is essential that you consider this in terms of how it will affect your retirement plan, which is what this chapter will discuss.

Erase from your mind the notion that you have to make more money to be wealthy and to have everything you want. You may very well need to make more to meet your goals, but you do not necessarily have to make the most amount of money to be wealthy.

No matter how much money you make, if you spend every penny of it, you will never be wealthy. People that live in that mansion in the community next to yours may not actually be any better off than you are. Although they make more money per year, they likely have larger and much more expensive debts to pay. People like to increase not just the amount of their paycheck but also the amount of money going out. This does not make them wealthy; it only puts them in a higher income bracket.

What you want, as someone planning to retire early, is not to make more money and have lots of money coming in, but to be wealthy. A wealthy person has many opportunities for success, and they are living at a higher level of freedom then those that make more and spend more.

WHAT IS YOUR NET WORTH?

A good place to start is to know what your net worth is. Net worth is a simple calculation of how much a person owns when all debts are subtracted from this. In other words, add up all the values of your assets, including your house, your stocks, and any possessions that you have of value (include your investments here). Then, subtract away all the debt that you have, including credit cards, your mortgage, and any other money you owe.

Your net worth can help you see just where you stand in terms of your financial goals. Are you living above your means? Are you living at a lower means than you need to?

To be wealthy, you must increase your net worth so that you own much more than you owe.

Net worth changes, and it changes as often as the balance of your accounts moves up and down. While you do not need to know this number all the time, for your retirement planning, you will want to see a steady increase in your net worth over time. That means you are building wealth, and that is a tool that will serve you well later on, too.

LIVE OFF YOUR AFTER-TAX INCOME

Many financial experts believe that those that can live off the after tax income they get from their investments are the true definition of wealthy. If you can obtain this goal, you too will be able to say you are wealthy.

Many people that are rich and well off never really touch their capital from their investments, but enjoy benefits from the actual income of that investment. Here is an example to consider.

Ken and Lisa realized that they would need about $70,000 per year during retirement to live the life style that they wanted to live. They had $900,000 invested in taxable accounts. They did not have any debt when they retired and had no use for it either. At an 8 percent rate of return, this investment allowed them to bring in an income of $72,000 per year, enough to pay for every expense they had during that year.

When you have to really use the capital of your investment, you lessen the amount of income that investment can provide you in the long run. If you only had $800,000 instead of $900,000, this would be a huge difference in terms of what the future would hold for that investment. It may not be able to produce nearly the same amount for you.

In turn, you can see that Ken and Lisa were able to have an

extra $2,000 that first year. (They actually did not spend all $70,000 either.) Nevertheless, they are able to take that extra income and reinvest it so that they are earning even more than they need to.

There is no doubt that this will not always be the case. Inflation will increase your expenses and problems will arise in your plan. Yet when you are able to compensate for this through reinvestments and good planning, you will be able to handle this additional cost. Even when you do need to use your capital eventually, by that time it should be all right to do so if you have planned well before then.

Another factor to consider is this: As you grow older, money is more difficult to earn in other forms. For example, if, at 50 years old, you lose a huge amount of money on the stock market, you may be able to go back to work to make up for this loss, in the worst case scenario. But, as you age, your level of risk tolerance will lower, and you will be less likely to invest in the most volatile of markets. You will want to invest less in risky situations and more in safer investments.

BALANCING DESIRES

A key element in putting yourself in a rewarding situation later in life is making some sacrifices now. Ask yourself the all important question: "Is what I want from this money today going to be worth the sacrifice that it causes down the road?"

There are some situations that will cause you to sacrifice

some money. Making the right choices today will help you achieve more later.

What you need is to focus on the long term when making decisions today. Not every decision is going to be retirement altering, but some will. The best ways to prevent problems are to do the following:

1. Save your money as much as you can. Save even more than that.

2. Invest well with educated, calculated decisions.

3. Manage your money well.

4. Be active in monitoring the progress your money makes for you.

5. Reassess your situation so that in the long term and short term, your goals are realized.

When you accomplish these goals, you will put yourself in the best position possible now and in retirement.

UNDERSTANDING YOUR RISK TOLERANCE

Now is a great time to discuss the conditions of your risk. In any situation, risk will help you know where you stand.

Here we discuss several important considerations that you must take into account. We will go into more detail about the specifics in later chapters, but understanding your risk tolerance will help you with gauging where your investments stand today.

In blackjack, the basic premise of the game is simple: The more you wager, the more you can win. But this also increases how much money you can potentially lose. The trick to the game, then, is to find a balance between how much you are willing to lose and how much you want to win — and, of course, making bigger bets when your chances of winning are higher.

This is not to say that saving for retirement should be a gamble of casino proportions, but much like gambling, investing for your future and deciding where your hard-earned money will work the best for you is a game of risk and reward. You have to determine how much you want to earn and how comfortable you are with the risks you are taking to get there.

All sources of retirement income are important to your overall retirement security, but savings and investments are the piece of the picture that you can design and over which you have the most control. How your principal and earnings grow to become a nest egg will depend not only on how much you put aside annually during your working years, but also on the investment decisions you make during this time.

When you invest, you are taking a chance and putting your dollars at risk. The outcome can be a loss or a gain. Potential return on an investment can be current income (such as interest, dividends, or rent and/or capital gains (in which an investment has increased or appreciated in value). The combination of income and capital gains is the total return from an investment. Not all your investment choices have the same potential for return. Savings accounts, involving almost no risk, often earn less than money invested in a mutual fund. Investing in individual stocks involves even more risk. This is the nature of the risk-return relationship. Those who want higher returns must accept greater risk.

In the financial world, your return on an investment can be influenced by several sources of uncertainty or risk.

TYPES OF RISK

- **Financial risk** is related to the financial health of a company and the possibility the investment will fail to pay a return to the investor.

- **Market risk** is the uncertainty that results from outside factors, such as economic, social, or political events, might impact the securities market.

- **Inflation risk** is the result of an increase in the prices of goods and services. To maintain the same purchasing power, returns on an investment must exceed the inflation rate.

- **Marketability risk** is the possibility of absorbing a loss if the investor is forced to sell an investment that is illiquid and cannot easily be converted to cash.

While it is impossible for an investor to control all risk, there are strategies an individual investor can use to reduce risk and feel more comfortable with their investments. The following chart lists investments in terms of the risk associated with them. In general, they are listed from least risky to those that involve the greatest risk.

LEVEL 1: LEAST RISK, LEAST RETURN.	• Certificates of deposit
	• Insured savings accounts
	• Money market accounts
	• Mutual funds
	• U.S. savings bonds
	• U.S. Treasury bills, bonds, and notes
LEVEL 2: LOWER RISK, LOWER RETURN.	• High-grade common stocks/stock mutual funds
	• High-grade corporate bonds/bond mutual funds
	• Life insurance cash values and fixed annuities
	• Preferred stocks/stock mutual funds
LEVEL 3: GREATER RISK, GREATER RETURN.	• Limited partnerships
	• Real estate investment properties
	• Speculative bonds/bond mutual funds
	• Speculative common stocks/stock mutual funds
LEVEL 4: GREATEST RISK, GREATEST RETURN.	• Collectables
	• Commodities
	• Options and "derivatives"
	• Precious metals

DIVERSIFICATION

How do you manage this risk? Ultimately, you want to make as much money from your investments, but the risk of losing it all holds you back. The tool for managing risk is diversification. This allows you to put your investment dollars into a variety of investment methods, spreading the risk out.

There are several methods to doing just that. Here are a few examples:

- You should split your savings and investments and put them in various places, such as money market accounts, certificates of deposit, individual stocks, bonds, mutual funds, and real estate.

- You should split your stock investments into large company stocks, small company stocks, international stocks, blue-chip stocks, and growth stocks.

- You should split your stock investments into different areas, such as utilities, energy, technology, financial, transportation, and health care.

There are many other methods that can be used. This flexibility allows everyone to find the ideal fit.

To manage all these risk considerations, your total investment package, called an investment portfolio, must be divided among the various types of investments you have. Your investment portfolio is divided, then, by asset allocation, or the method of selecting the right portion of your portfolio for each category.

A common option is a 20/20/40 portfolio in which 20 percent of the portfolio is stocks (high risk), 40 percent of the portfolio is bonds (less risk), and the remaining 40 percent is cash (no risk). This will change from one person to the next depending on their level of risk tolerance. You must also consider your goals here. How much time do you have until you retire? How much do you need to earn before then?

DEFINE WHERE YOU STAND

An essential part of managing your portfolio is comparing your goals to your abilities to risk money. Most people are part of one of three categories that help to determine how their portfolio should be divided. There are shades of grey between each level, of course.

Conservative: A person considered conservative is one that is looking for safety. They are not interested in the ultimate pay day, but rather in knowing that what they have will remain theirs.

Moderate: In the middle of the road is a moderate investor. A moderate investor is willing to put some principal at risk, but not all. This investor is willing to take some risks (more than a conservative would) but not looking for a huge risk and possibility of financial return (as the aggressive would).

Aggressive: The ultimate investor that likes taking risks is that of the aggressive investor. Here, the only goal is to risk highly for the potential gain available by doing so.

Take the time to consider where you stand. While educated financial planners will be able to help you make the right decisions, there is never a guarantee that an aggressive investor will see a high return on investment. The question to ask, then, is what type of investment philosophy do you have?

ADDITIONAL FACTORS IN YOUR DECISION

There are other factors that play a role in where you place your money in your investment portfolio. One of those is time. How much time do you have until you retire? The shorter time you have the more conservative you need to be with your investments because you do not want to lose too much money. There is less time to make up for any loss you may suffer. For those with a longer amount of time, a more aggressive plan can help give you a higher return on investment. If there are drops in the value of your portfolio, this can be made up over time, without hurting your retirement strategy.

The sooner that you can plan your retirement the more likely it will be for you to take a more aggressive approach to investing and make potentially larger amounts of money.

Another factor is return needs. Earlier in this book, you were asked to consider your own financial needs during retirement. Your estimated retirement income needs and your time horizon will determine the target return you set for your portfolio. In setting this target, it is important to be realistic. For instance, if you have a very short time until retirement, it is unrealistic to expect huge returns with your low level of risk tolerance. It would then be imperative to either decide to postpone your retirement by a few years or to decide that you could potentially live on less income during retirement. In the last third of this book, we will discuss the many options available to those who wish to retire early, whether or not they feel they have the means to do so. Consider your own return needs and decide how that fits into your overall plan for early retirement.

BALANCE, BALANCE, BALANCE

In the end, your investment allocation should be unique to you and your situation and should not be a replica of anyone else's plan. Because it is determined by your own age, income, family situation, personal financial goals, and tolerance for risk, your investment plan should not be identical to that of your friends or family members.

With your goals in mind and an understanding of your comfort zone, your time horizon, and your target return, it is time to create your investment plan. Try to stay flexible and keep in mind that your plan should change as you get older and your financial situation changes.

At the earliest points in retirement planning, you can afford to be more aggressive to grow your retirement nest egg. Because your goal at this time is merely to grow your funds for retirement, the most important thing is to grow your investments quickly. Because the length of time until your retirement is greater at this point, you are able to take on more risk by investing in stocks and bonds that have a higher rate of return than some lower-risk endeavors.

When you get a bit closer to retirement, it is prudent to take on less risk, by moving some of your funds into lower-risk savings accounts. This not only liquefies more of your resources, but helps to preserve more of your principal investment. This will become increasingly important as you age and as your annual income needs grow with the onset of greater medical bills and higher life insurance rates.

Early in your retirement, you will begin to spend some of your capital on living expenses. Your assets will need to last you throughout the rest of your retirement years — which, if you succeed in retiring early, could be a very long time — potentially 40 or 50 years. So, it is important to remember that not all your retirement funds will be needed at once. Part of your investment can continue to grow. At this time, you will want to keep some of your money invested in stocks so that your investment earnings will keep up with the rate of inflation.

Later in retirement, it is likely that your health expenses will increase with age, resulting in a need for more income. At this point, however, you will be able to access your retirement accounts without penalty, so more of your assets will be liquefied. You will still want to keep a smaller portion of your assets in stocks and bonds to continue ensuring that the return on your investment will keep up with the rate of inflation throughout the end of your retirement.

IT IS NOT SET IN STONE

It is just as important to consider your investment portfolio down the road as it is today. Your needs as well as your investment philosophy are likely to change over time. As part of your retirement plan, you must come back, look at, and make changes to your asset allocation to put it in the best position for that time moving forward. It can be important to do this every year.

CHAPTER

6

WEALTH — YOU CAN GET THERE

Regardless of your current income, you have the financial ability to retire early if you work for it. This means controlling spending and living below your means. To build a retirement nest egg, you will need to spend less than you earn and build up savings over many years to provide income and financial security for your life after retirement.

Living below your means is the most effective tool for finding the cash that you need to save for retirement. In practice, living below your means should resemble sensible and frugal discipline rather than deprivation. It is important to buy what you need and to have some fun, but you should also understand that you cannot expect to buy everything that you want. You have to ensure that your finances are not squandered through careless and impulsive expenditure of your resources.

There are some people who seem to be naturally good at saving. Living below their means is seemingly second nature. These people are great at organizing their budgets in such a way that keeping expenses in check becomes easy and natural. But for those who are not among these lucky few, living below their means is another chore in which they must resist the temptation to spend money.

If you are just beginning to plan for retirement, you will first need to become better at saving. Right now, it might seem that your paycheck cannot keep up with the endless list of demands that you put on it. But if you buckle down and begin to develop a healthier savings, you will not only find that living life now becomes easier, but that your nest egg for the future will grow exponentially.

The decisions you make regarding your family's spending are personal and unique to your situation. The approach you choose to develop a healthy pattern of spending must fit the budget, preferences, and life style of you and your family. This guide is meant to help you along the way. The key to living below your means is creating a budget that you can live with and live by. These are the ingredients that go into the development of a successful budget.

CAN YOU LIVE WITH IT?

Budgeting your spending is a lot like dieting. If you do not create a budget that you can live with, it will be difficult to stick with it. There is no point, then, in setting goals that you will not be able to keep. So, set target budget goals that force you to make decisions about your spending, but that are not impossible to live with.

Like dieting, the goal of budgeting is to feel good about

what you have achieved, rather than feeling guilty about where you have fallen short of your goals, so make sure that your goals are achievable.

CAN YOU KEEP TRACK OF IT?

While it is not necessary to obsess about every penny, keeping track of your budget is a good way to keep yourself on track. This is a no-brainer. By writing down your expenditures, or keeping track of them some other way, you will be able to see exactly where your money is going and identify potential spending leaks before they become a problem.

Somewhere in your budget, be sure to identify your needs and your wants, so that if spending leaks gets out of hand, you can easily find ways to cut back and get back on track.

There are a plethora of computer programs on the market that promise to help you track your spending. Quicken and Microsoft Money are the most popular. You do not have to spend money on a fancy computer program to keep track of your spending, though. In most instances, the ledger in the back of your checkbook or a spreadsheet program can help. There are many tools that you can use to create a budget and keep track of your spending so that you know where you need to tighten your belt a bit further. Find the method of keeping track of your spending that works best for you and stick with it for a positive budget experience.

CAN EVERYONE AGREE?

Compromise is the most important part of any relationship, and this is especially important to remember in regard to financial matters.

Disagreements regarding money account for more divorces every year than any other marital problem. Understanding this potentially explosive situation, it is important to receive input from your spouse when creating a spending plan. If you are in a relationship of any kind, it is imperative that you work out spending and saving goals together. By developing ways to implement your plan that work for both parties, you can ensure that you stay on track in your finances and your relationship.

Work together to control spending and savings just as you would work together to improve any other aspect of your relationship. Only together can you overcome your obstacles and celebrate your achievements to set yourselves up for financial success in the future.

JUST DO IT

If the very idea of a budget makes you cringe, chances are you are among those who think that a budget is too restrictive or limiting. But rather than assuming that it will take the fun out of life by controlling your spending, it is helpful to see it as a focal point. That is, a budget helps you focus on purchasing the items that bring you the most financial and personal reward. If designed and followed through effectively, a good budget is meant to put you in control of your expenses, rather than letting your expenses control you.

GATHERING INFORMATION FOR A BUDGET

To successfully prepare and use a budget, you will need to plan for the expected and unexpected by monitoring, controlling, and reevaluating your finances. Do this by first gathering all your financial records — bank statements, pay stubs, and the like (everything that you would gather to prepare your income taxes). This is a good place to begin because you keep these documents around anyway. What you must do is determine your real income — that is, what you actually bring home after taxes and purchased benefits, plus any interest, dividend, rental, or royalty income that you earn.

Income is any type of money that comes into your home. Here are some possible sources:

- What are your regular paychecks from your employment?

- If you are not working, are you receiving unemployment benefits?

- Are you receiving any bonus payments from your employment, a side business, or otherwise?

- Are you receiving income from investments that you have, including your savings account?

- Are you getting Social Security benefits or any other type of public assistance?

- Do you receive any help for caring for your child from the government, from a spouse, or anyone else?

- Do you receive any income from rental property or other assets that you own?

In addition to this, you will need to determine your fixed outflow. This includes all your household expenditures that occur regularly: rent/mortgage, gas/electric, water, phone/cable/Internet, property taxes/insurance, car payments/insurance, and anything else that you pay on a monthly or quarterly basis. Do not include your expenses that change from one week to the next, however, such as food and entertainment. These will be determined through your own monitoring of expense.

When you know your income and outflow, you will want to subtract the outflow from the income and find the remainder. This remainder is the amount of income that you have available for variable outflow — your food, entertainment, and occasional expenses, but also your savings and investment.

DETERMINE YOUR MONTHLY EXPENSES

When you know what your income is and what your necessary outflow is, you can begin to tweak your budget. No two homes are completely the same; therefore, you must create your own spending needs based on your family, not someone else's.

There are some helpful tools that should be used to help you determine what your estimated costs should be. These are based on what other people in similar income and economic situations are facing. You will use these to help determine where your expense goal should be.

A key element in this is your shelter. Rent or mortgage, your home's insurance, and your taxes should be your largest expense. It is recommended that this be between 25 and 30 percent of your income. From here, the next 25 to 30 percent should be towards your other fixed expenses as listed previously.

As you can see, this only accounts for about half the income that you should bring into your home. The rest of that income should go to expenses that fluctuate, as well as your savings and investments. Most financial planners will tell you that at least 10 percent of your income should go toward your savings.

This still leaves you with a considerable chunk of money. More than likely, you do not have your current needs in these percentage goals so that extra will work to help you adjust. What is more, you may not have an average amount of expenses for some reason. This still leaves plenty of adjustment room.

Your goal is to try to put yourself in a position in which your budget closely resembles this situation. Plus or minus some, the end result is to know how much you will spend on each piece of your budget using your income every month.

When you do this, you allow for a spending plan that works for you and your family. It gives a specific goal for each month, and it allows you to make changes when necessary. You should incorporate things like going to the movies or buying what you want, but it should still be budgeted. For example, perhaps a family entertainment budgeted amount is added to accommodate for things like those expenses.

TWEAKING TO PERFECTION

It is very likely that you will need to tweak your budget (and perhaps your income) to fit with your retirement savings goals. Ultimately, you want to have income to meet all of your goals, including that of your investment needs. Adjusting your spending habits is one way to do that.

The question to ask is, "What can I cut back on?" From here, explore things like the grocery budget, the entertainment fund, and money spent on eating out. The most important expenses that should not go unpaid are your housing and insurance, but you may be able to cut them down.

It may be necessary, at some point, to increase your income. This happens for many people, at least until debts like credit cards and car loans can be paid off. Realize that this may not be a long-term need but a need until you can get caught up.

Saving by cutting back has the most potential for most people. How can you cut back? Here are some areas to look into.

FOOD AND HOUSEHOLD EXPENSES

Decrease the amount of times you eat out, create a monthly meal plan, and buy groceries that are on sale. Cut back on the prepared foods and make more fresh meals. Base your meals on what is on sale or on hand. Do not go shopping more than you need to; once a week is good. Cut down on impulse buys by shopping with a grocery list only. Find out if there are any low cost grocery stores available in your area. Look for off brand products.

MAINTAINING YOUR HOME

Be sure to do preventative maintenance on your home's appliances to keep them running smoothly as directed in your owner's manual. Change filters, repair damaged windows and doors, and when upgrading appliances, look for energy saving options. Reduce your air conditioning as much as possible in summer and the heat in the winter and instead wear appropriate clothing. Turn off lights and appliances when not in use.

TRANSPORTATION

Keep your car running at its best by providing regularly scheduled maintenance check ups. Car pool to work. Plan errands and do them all at one time. Try taking public transportation instead of driving when possible. Update your car insurance yearly with a new quote that may be less expensive. Drive vehicles that are paid for instead of financed.

MEDICAL EXPENSES

Keep yourself healthy by getting exercise and eating well. Have the right amount of health insurance to cover most needs. Get help at the soonest possible instance of illness rather than waiting until complications arise. Use preventative elements in your home to keep children safe. Look for affordable insurance products that are able to cover everyone's need. Use generic drugs instead of name brands.

ENTERTAINMENT

Cut back on spending by doing more free or sponsored activities in your city. Explore the public parks, bike ride, and go fishing. Take advantage of religious groups, community groups, and the library for movies, CDs, and books.

CARING FOR CHILDREN

Child care can be made less expensive if you find someone in your neighborhood, a relative, or a friend that can offer care at a discounted price. Look for a playgroup or other activities. Find out if your employer offers any child care discounts or benefits. Look to your local government for low cost options.

MAKE YOUR SPENDING PLAN FUNCTION

Your spending plan or budget is an important part of all the work you are doing for it. Just writing it out does not make it happen. You must guide the spending decisions that you make each month by the budget you have designed.

For example, if you budget $500 a month to use as you see fit for entertainment and eating out, spending $600 is not acceptable. While you may have 101 excuses to do just that, it does not help if you go over the limit. In emergency situations, this may be important, but for a situation like this, it simply does not make sense to your long-term goals.

Yes, that means saying no to some of the things that you want to do or finding less expensive ways to do them. The underlying result, though, is that your budget keeps you on track to achieving your financial goals, something that will reward you throughout your entire life.

REASSESS OFTEN ENOUGH

A key to finding a good place to put yourself financially is to be sure that you are taking a good, hard look at yourself.

Knowing where you stand allows you to make changes and allows you to find the right position for yourself in the long term. You see what needs done and can take action to correct it. Looking at yourself like this allows you to see not only where you need to make changes, but also to see the progress that you made. It is encouraging and motivating and can move you past where you are and into success.

Reassessing where you stand is a key element that must be determined every three months at the start and every six to nine months down the road.

THE DEBT ISSUE

Debt is one of the biggest problems for people that are trying their best to save for retirement. You can overcome it.

It is certainly difficult to think about saving for your future while you are still paying for your past. But to consider retiring early you must find a way to pay down your debt and invest in your future. Debt is a fetter to your financial security and freedom, and until you are able to undo the negative effects it has on your life, you can never truly feel free, even after retirement.

For that reason, it is essential that you tackle that debt monster now, while there is still the likelihood that you can overcome it. The sooner you do so, the better and brighter the future will be for you.

Step 1: Figure Out How Much Debt You Really Have

The first step to removing debt from your life is to learn

how much you really have and the effects that it is having on your life. When you are more aware of exactly how much debt you have and what it is doing to you — your stress level, your relationships, your family, and your life — you can begin working to eradicate it.

Begin by pulling out all your bills and figuring out your total indebtedness. Write it all down in one place to help you keep track — include the names of lenders, the total amount you owe, the minimum payment that is due each month, and the interest rate that you are paying on each account. A great way to do this is to use an Excel spreadsheet, which will allow you to input all your debt accounts, followed by the amount you owe. You can also use this tool to help you to keep track of payments and interest. This can ultimately help you pay off your debt quickly.

Prioritize Your Payments

While it is important to pay all your bills regularly to eradicate your debt and improve your credit, when push comes to shove, there are always some bills that are more important than others.

The most important things are those things that you cannot live without, such as your housing and your utilities. You need to be able to get to work, to feed your family, and to keep them insured. Anything that you need to live should be the first bills you pay.

The second consideration has to do with the IRS. If you owe them money, the best bet is to pay them. The last thing that you need is costly fees for being late or not filing a return. Government backed loans need to be paid back or they will come after you.

What is left over will be paid last. That includes any credit cards that you have, payments for entertainment expenses, and anything else that does not fit in the above categories.

Your goal will be to stay current on all debts you have, large and small. This means taking the time necessary to make decisions regarding the importance of each of those items. Doing this allows you to prioritize where your money goes when it comes in.

Step 2: Track Your Spending

As mentioned, you need to track your spending through a budget. If you did not create one yet, do so. Now, you have one goal in mind: Balance it. But you also want to look for ways to cut down on what you owe so that you can put yourself in a better situation.

Tracking your spending is also a good source of finding out what you actually are spending money on. Here is how to go about finding this cost.

Give each person that uses your household budget a small pad of paper. This pad should be kept with them. Anytime that any purchase is made, write down that purchase. This should include all those stops for ice cream after the soccer game, the purchase of a can of soda at work, and even the cost of your morning coffee.

Be sure that if you use credit cards you also include the purchases that you made on credit. This is essential so that you know what you are actually spending, not just spending cash on.

You do not need to be critical of yourself at this point. Spend the next month doing this, and you will clearly see where your money is going. Then, categorize your purchases:

- **Essentials** — Utilities, mortgage payment, car payments, and the like

- **Revolving Debt** — Credit cards, other loan payments

- **Household Expenses** — Food, bathroom essentials, must-haves for the home

- **Eating Out** — Any meal outside the home, including snacks

- **Entertainment** — Movie money, money spent on toys

- **Home Improvements** — Repairs and purchases for the home

Take a close look at all your purchases. Add up the totals for each of the categories and see where you are. You can easily see where you need to make cuts when you do this.

This exercise should be done while cutting down credit because you will need to trim as many categories as you can so that you can put extra money toward your debt. That is the next step.

Step 3: Stop Spending on Credit

A key element to paying down debt is to stop creating it. While that may seem like a challenge it is ultimately the best way to stop paying people to use your own money.

Consider this example. Vicky is a great mom and likes to manage her money. She pays off a credit card and says she does not need to use it again. But now she does not have any cash to use so she resorts to using that card to purchase something. The problem is the $10 toy she buys for her son will end up costing her $12, $13, or more by the time she actually pays off that credit card again.

While she had the money to buy the toy and only pay $10 for it, she used credit and now has to pay more.

You need to keep your budget organized and pay off your debts only when you have funded the rest of your budget as well.

Do not keep adding to your credit either. If you continue to use it, you will never get it paid off. Instead, put them aside and learn to live off the cash budget that you have created for yourself. At this point, only concentrate on paying the minimums on your credit card debt until you can get each of your categories organized. Set aside money for each of the items in your budget to use as you see fit.

While it may be easy to put aside money in your budget for

your mortgage, you may be leery of budgeting for things that seem more unnecessary, such as entertainment or money that can be used on anything you deem important. Yet, by having these additional amounts in your budget, you can cut down on the number of times you will need to resort to credit to make a purchase.

The best tool to keep you from using your credit cards is not to have them. If you feel that they are a security blanket for you for emergency situations, put them away in a locked box or even a safety deposit at your bank.

Once you stop using credit and depending on it, you will quickly find yourself able to pay down your debts faster.

Step 4: Deal with Your Credit Cards

Paying off your debt is the goal, but how can you do that if all you are making is minimum payments? You will not be able to do so at this rate. You need to do more than just make minimum payments on the loans you have; otherwise, you will pay on them for ten or more years.

What can you do, then?

There are several solutions. First, start by getting yourself caught up on your bills. You should not be behind on any of them. This will help you get the ball rolling because it helps you stop paying too much in late fees and over the limit fees.

Once you are caught up, structure all your debts in terms of what you owe on them. Here we are not concerned with your mortgage or your car payments, but revolving debt, as this has the highest interest rates on it and therefore is the largest debt you have. It is the most important thing for you to tackle before you can begin planning your retirement.

List your debts in a spreadsheet or even a piece of paper starting with the smallest balance and ending with the largest. You may be wondering why you would not start by paying off the largest debt you have. The answer is in terms of your building power.

When you pay as much as you can after allowing every category in your budget to get to the lowest balance, you are likely to pay it off within just a few months. For example, if you have a credit card that has a balance of $500 and you can put $300 from your budget to your debt, this small balance would be paid off fastest. Not only do you still have that $300 to move on to the next highest balance, but you also have the minimum payment on that first credit card to put towards the next one. So, if the minimum payment you have to make every month is $50 on the $500 credit line, once it is paid off, you can put $350 toward your next debt.

If that next debt is a credit card has a $700 balance and a monthly payment of $60, you can pay it off in just a few short months by putting the $350 toward it. Then, the next credit card has $410 toward it and so on.

You will want to do this while maintaining those other monthly payments. As discussed, balance your budget first. Then, anything extra should go toward your debt.

Keep paying off your credit cards every month in this fashion until you are paid off completely.

Pay More Than the Minimum Payments

Why not just keep paying your minimum payments until they are paid off? Unfortunately, most credit cards will have a high enough interest rate that any minimum payment you make is going to only be a fraction of what the finance charges will be on that credit card. For example, have you ever noticed on your statement that the $30 minimum payment only seems to bring the balance that you owe down by under $10? The next month you are still paying another $30, but your balance does not seem to drop by much.

In many cases, you can spend years paying off your debt if you go about doing so like this.

Lower Your Interest Rates

What most people do not realize is that you can lower the interest rate you pay on your credit cards. To do so, pick up the phone and call your lenders.

If they are forced to make a decision about keeping a good customer or cutting your interest rate, they will do so. You can often do this any time, which means you should give them a call every few months.

For those that are unsure of what they should say to get a lower rate, here are some ideas:

- State how long you have been a customer with the company.

- State that you have never been late on a payment or that you have not been late on a payment for the last 12 months.

- State that you would like to keep using their service but that you are shopping for a lower interest rate.

- Be sure that they know that your credit score has been improving and that you have recently paid off X amount of money, credit cards, or other debts.

- Tell them of your plan to pay off your balance in full and that you will then make monthly payments that pay off the entire card down the road.

It is important to say that you need and want a lower interest rate to keep doing business with them. If you have two credit cards and one has a lower rate than the other, which one would you use? Use this information to your advantage. Be sure to let the credit card company know that you are using only credit lines that offer you the best rate possible.

Chances are good they will lower the interest that you pay. They will not do this, though, if you do not call and ask. They will continue to take advantage of you as long as you allow them to.

It is particularly important to call your lenders to ask for a lower rate if you are currently improving your credit score. Chances are good that you qualify for a lower rate if you improve your score by 20 points or more.

Step 5: Grow Your Income

The income that you have is an important part of your retirement plan, but it is also an essential part of paying off your debt. Remember that you are planning for your retirement and that means paying off the debt you owe, especially high interest rate credit cards.

Consider the facts. You likely pay between 10 and 25 percent interest on your credit cards or other unsecured loans. But the money that you have tucked away in a CD or other savings account is earning a mere 6 percent. Are you spending more than you are saving? Does it make sense to work on building your wealth like this if you have not first removed the most expensive things from your budget?

Some individuals will find it hard to pay off debt, though, especially if they have a lot of it. It is estimated that the average American household has between $7,000 and $10,000 of debt.

Paying it off is essential, but to pay it off you may have to increase your income. This is an essential part of analyzing your budget. If your budget lays out specific amounts that you will spend on various needs, it should include as much as possible being put toward your debt. Cutting corners and shaving off things that you do not need to spend money on is only one step. It may also be necessary to get additional work.

How can you improve your income? Here are some ideas:

- **Ask for a raise.** State your case in terms of how long you have been with the company. Do your research and find out what others with your education and experience are making. Present all the good things you have accomplished. Talk about your goals of working with the company long term.

- **Pick up additional hours.** For those that are working hourly or those that can do consulting work, this is a great way to increase your income. Talk to your boss or look for other positions that allow you to pick up a few extra hours here and there.

- **Decrease your retirement investments until you pay off your debt.** Instead of putting money away for the long term, pay off the debts that are costing you far more than you will earn in your 401(k).

Do what it takes to increase your income. Any money earned will be used to pay down debt. Remember, this is a short-lived need and that means that you will not need to do this long — just until your debt is repaid.

Step 6: Straighten It Out

Your credit report could be hurting you. Do you know what it is? If not, learn. Your credit report is a simple tool that is used by all lenders to determine if they should give you credit. This report is used to keep track of your borrowing habits. The goal is to keep other lenders from issuing credit to someone that does not deserve it.

Errors can happen often, though, which is why you must

take the time to learn what your score is and then work to improve any areas you can.

It is also very important to know your personal consumer credit score. The credit score is an actual number, whereas your credit report provides the detailed information. Both are very important. When you begin paying down your debt regularly, your credit score will rise, enabling you to get lower interest rates on your credit accounts.

Every consumer is entitled to one free credit report each year from each of the three credit bureaus — three total. The smart thing to do is to get one every four months; that way you can make sure you have not been a victim of identity theft.

To get a free report, you can go to the Web site set up by the Federal Trade Commission, **www.annualcredit report.com.**

If you cannot get a free report, you can buy one from one of the three credit-reporting agencies:

- Equifax: 888-766-0008 or **www.equifax.com**

- Experian: 888-397-3742 or **www.experian.com**

- TransUnion: 800-680-7289 or **www.transunion.com**

You will need to enter your personal information here, and identifying information will be displayed so that only you can open your credit file. When you do this, print off the copy it provides to you. Note any mistakes on the credit report, including:

- Mistakes in your name, address, or employer information

- Mistakes in the accounts that you have open in your name

- Mistakes in the credit reporting from those creditors; for example, mistakes with making payments on time

- Mistakes of any other nature

Each of the three credit bureaus allows you to make changes to your report by filing a claim with them. This can be done right on the Web or you can call them. Your goal should be to have as much information as possible backing up your claim so that you can be sure that everything there is an accurate representation of who you are.

As for your credit score, if you do want to see what this number is, you will need to "purchase" it from the credit bureaus. For those that have the means, credit monitoring can be a good thing because it will allow you to see your credit score rise and fall with the actions that you make.

Why does an accurate credit report and credit score matter in retirement planning? Everything you will ever need to purchase in terms of credit or credit lines will be based on your credit score. Virtually all aspects of your life revolve around this, including your ability to purchase a new car, a new home, and even getting a new job. For this reason, invest in finding out if everything on your report is accurate.

For the sake of early retirement, invest in working to build your credit score, but do not become obsessed about it. Remember that you are in the business of paying off your debt.

Tips for Raising Your Credit Score

There are many things that can be done to help you to raise your credit score. Here are some tips to use.

- **Make payments on time every month** — One late payment costs you considerably in credit score points.

- **Do not continue to use credit** — The lower your credit debt to credit limit balance is, the better.

- **Do not apply for many new credit lines** — This can cause your credit score to drop because it looks like you are desperate for credit.

- **Do make payments on your home on time** — Secured debts are essential for establishing a good credit score.

- **Work at using credit responsibly** — If and when you use credit, always pay off the balance of your credit card every month.

Raising your credit score will help you to afford more of what you want from the rest of your life. Remember, by paying off debt, you have more money available to do the things that you want to with it, like investing in your early retirement.

Step 7: Understand Your Credit

One of the final steps in improving your debt situation so that you can fund your retirement is to know why you shop. Unfortunately, you may be shopping for emotional reasons.

Many people enjoy shopping because it is a way for them to break away from the stresses of life and get something nice for themselves or those that they love. If you are someone that feels the need to shop even though there is nothing you need, it could be that shopping is doing more for you than just providing you with necessities.

For example, do you walk into a mall and enjoy going from store to store purchasing things you may not need or even want? Or do you simply spend beyond your budget and then are unsure of what you purchased? This is quite common, and it is likely to be a real problem for you emotionally and financially.

When you have emotional trouble connecting with the shopping you are doing, it is going to hurt your future retirement goals. Spending money is not going to help you build a future early retirement. Is this worth an argument between you and your spouse? Perhaps it is time to work through why you shop and not just how much you spend.

Getting through that emotional baggage really can help you save money, and it allows you to make better decisions regarding your hard earned money. Learn what is really behind your shopping habits.

Step 8: Build Savings

Throughout the entire process, you will need to consider your ability to save money. It is essential to build an emergency fund that will be used to pay for emergency situations. For many, the problem with credit is that it is available where cash may not be. When something goes wrong, you may quickly see the problem of paying for a purchase with credit. Yet if you have savings put aside, you should be able to take care of most issues when they arise and not have to resort to credit to pay for it.

For example, Amy's vehicle broke down, and although she was planning on paying off her next credit card this month, she now has to use a credit card to pay for the car repair. But if she had an emergency fund put in place, she could have used those funds, repaid them, and then paid off her credit card a month or so later.

Therefore, your first goal should be to establish a small emergency fund of about $1,000 to $2,000 that can be used in times of real need. This should not be used for expenses such as entertainment or purchasing something for the home. You should build this amount up as quickly as possible before you begin paying off your debt.

After you pay off your credit cards, the next step is to build up a larger emergency fund, which should amount to three to six month's worth of expenses. These funds should not be invested in any way that is overly risky, and they should be available within a few short days if needed.

Later this book will discuss more investment opportunities, but for now, the goal is to pay off debt. Do not invest heavily if you have not paid off at least high interest rate debt. The cost of this debt is not made up through your investment.

PROTECT YOUR INCOME

Now that you have a plan for getting out of debt and you have the ability to build up a savings account for emergency situations, the next goal is to protect your income. To do that, you must start by looking at the situations in which even large amounts of emergency money will not help you.

The risks that you take in terms of your income do not have to be solely managed by you. You may be able to put yourself in a better position financially if you let another person or company, namely insurance companies, take on the risks that are now involved.

Insurance agencies make their money by providing you with help in paying for large problems because they know it is rare that most people will face these situations. Nevertheless, it is incredibly possible that something bad could happen. So, instead of taking on that risk, let an insurance company do the work for you.

Insurance is broken down into categories based on what it protects. You should have several types of insurance to help with your needs. Here is a quick look at some of the insurance products you must invest in, when possible, to help protect you.

DISABILITY INSURANCE

People between the ages of 25 and 55 are twice as likely to become disabled for 90 days or more than they are to die during this time. Therefore, you must protect yourself from being unable to work.

If you think that you do not need disability insurance, ask yourself, "What would happen to my family if I could not work?" The answer to that question is likely to be that you would tap into your emergency savings, and when that would run dry, you would be in a real problem financially. Most important, could you maintain the life style that you are currently living without having the ability to work?

For most people that answer is no, and that is where disability insurance comes into play. Every adult that earns an income should have disability insurance for the protection of the household.

You can purchase disability insurance through your local insurance agency. You may also be able to save money on this policy by bundling it with other insurance products. It is essential for you to realize the type of insurance you are getting. Therefore, work closely with your insurance agent to choose the right policy for your family's needs. You should feel good about having this type of insurance to lessen the risks for you and your family.

LIFE INSURANCE

If you are providing for your family, you also need life insurance. Life insurance lessens the financial strain that your family will endure if something were to happen to you and you were to die. Some people may not need life insurance, especially those that do not have dependants. If other people depend on your income, though, you do need to have this insurance.

Life insurance policies range greatly. Again, having a professional help you is the best route to take in choosing the right policy. Work closely with them to understand what your real need is, as well as how much you can afford. They will present various types of policies to you, and it will take some work to find the right one, but in the end, it provides the protection that is right for you and your family.

PROPERTY INSURANCE, CASUALTY INSURANCE

Two other types of insurance products to consider are property insurance and casualty insurance, which often go hand in hand. Your home is a large part of your investment and often provides the most security in a time of crisis by giving you equity. Yet if something were to destroy it, such as a fire, that security would be gone, along with quite a bit of your hard earned money.

Property insurance provides you with necessary protection, but it must be thorough. You should have a policy that covers the cost of rebuilding your home and the cost of replacing your home's contents. Any property that you own should have this amount of protection on it. If you do provide this, be sure that it is kept up to date with the value of your home today, not what it was five or ten years ago.

HEALTH INSURANCE

We have talked about how important health insurance is down the road, after you retire, but it is just as important right now. Without health insurance, an illness or a sudden injury can leave you and your family in financial ruin. This would surely destroy the plans you are making for an early retirement.

The cost of health care today continues to rise, which means there is a large need to have comprehensive coverage. But what should you have? There are several products available, and your insurance agent can help you find the right policy for your needs.

Many people get insurance through their place of employment, but find out what is covered and if enough is covered. Your children, spouse, and any other dependants you have should be covered by as well. Having this coverage can help you pay for routine medical check ups, as well as those unexpected events that will likely happen at some point during your life.

Be sure that everyone you are responsible for has health insurance, and that it is enough to provide comprehensive, long-term protection.

UMBRELLA COVERAGE

For everything else there is umbrella coverage. If someone were to have an accident on your property or your car was involved in an accident and your homeowners and auto insurance policies did not cover it, this policy would. It provides the help you need to really protect everything and anything that could happen.

You should have a million dollar umbrella policy that will cover anything that every other type of insurance does not cover. Talk to your insurance agent about this type of coverage and your needs for it. Chances are good they will have several recommendations for you.

Regardless of what you believe your future will hold, no one can know for sure what it does hold. Therefore, having insurance to help take away some of that risk is vitally important to your daily life but also to your retirement plan. When your retirement plan is in place and making money for you, you do not want anything to get in the way of that. More so, if something should, you want there to be coverage that will take care of the problem without costing you a small fortune. By getting this type of help, you can protect yourself and your family from all "the what if" situations that are out there.

CHAPTER

7 YOU ARE A MILLIONAIRE IN TRAINING

T he key is to making money is to live like a millionaire would live, but without actually spending like they do

It is easy to figure out that you will need — say just under a million dollars. Much more difficult is the task of imagining how that money might materialize between now and the day that you plan on retiring, especially when you want that day to come sooner rather than later. So, it is time to begin thinking outside the box.

START EARLY

Regardless of how old you are right now, it is time to begin planning and saving for your future. If you have children, now would be a good time to begin planning for their futures as well. There is no such thing as beginning to plan for your retirement too early.

If you look at saving for your retirement as the path to

buying your freedom from the daily grind, it is easy to see why it should be such a priority. And the greater you would like that freedom to be, the earlier you should begin preparing for it — especially if you want that chapter of your life to begin as early as possible (while you are still young enough to enjoy it). So, when you have drawn the picture of what you would like your retirement to look like and considered the cost of that goal, it is time to begin finding sources of funding for your goals. If your future involves money, time can only be your friend.

If you happen to be 20 years old while reading this book, good for you. Do not walk, run to your nearest bank and deposit $50 into a savings account. Do that every week once a week until you graduate from college. If you can part with $200 a month ($2,400/each year) from the age of 20 through adulthood, investing that money at a 10 percent rate of return, you can be a millionaire by the age of 60.

For those of you who do not have the luxury of being in your 20s while reading this book, take solace in the fact that all hope is not lost; retirement just might cost you a little more to get where you want to be. It is much easier to begin planning for a retirement that is far into the distant future than one that is only five or even ten years away.

For this reason, it is important to use your resources and your time wisely.

Your resources include your credit, your income, and your current savings. By putting these resources to work for you over time, you can ensure that your retirement nest egg is there, ready and waiting for you on the day you retire. You can develop a decent-sized savings with little resources and a larger amount of time or else with larger resources if you have less time available to you. But it will be difficult to develop a savings with no resources or time, due to the fact that your money must be given time to grow.

Time is the single most critical factor when considering retirement savings. If you begin saving for retirement at the age of 20 — before even graduating from college — time provides much more opportunity than if you were to wait ten years. If you begin investing $2,400 each year for ten years, beginning at the age of 20, you will have invested only $24,000 by the time you are 30. Then, even if you choose to invest nothing more, you will find that at the age of 50, your money has grown into a lump sum of just over $257,000. However, if you waited until the age of 30, you would have to invest just under $4,500 each year for 20 years to reach the same goal.

The beauty of compound interest is the way in which you can see your money feed upon itself and grow over time. It is possible, then, for your money to grow to the amount that you need it when you need it. Through compound interest, your initial principal and subsequent deposits earn interest and the interest that your account earns will earn interest as well, thus allowing your money to compound upon itself.

There is no one right way to save for retirement. Consider what will work for you and your situation. Keep in mind that the less time you have between the time you begin saving and the time you retire, the more you will have to save during each period to achieve your target lump sum.

Time is the single most important ingredient for the creation of wealth. This is because any small amount of money you save today can grow to a decent-sized nest egg for the future. But also, if you have less time available to save, you can see that it is possible to do so by making larger payments.

Now that you understand how compound interest can work for you, you must also know the work that you will have to do to save money for investment.

KEEP TRACK OF YOUR SPENDING

By understanding your current spending patterns, you will be able to keep track of your necessary and unnecessary expenditures. Try keeping a record of your household expenses, and write a spending plan to budget for your occasional unnecessary expenses. The written plan will help you see where your money is going, and it will help you curb frivolous spending so that you can invest more money in your future. To save more, you will need to be able to identify your spending leaks — those little expenses that have become habitual and add up over time.

For Lyn, her biggest spending leak, for instance, was the daily trip to the local coffee shop for café mocha. At $4 a cup, 5 days a week, however, that adds up to $20 a week, or $80 each month. By cutting down the gourmet coffee habit to two days a week, she is able to invest an extra $48 each month into future retirement. This will add up. An additional $576 invested each year until retirement could potentially add tens of thousands of dollars to a retirement nest egg.

Perhaps you do not particularly enjoy coffee, but it is likely that you have some spending leaks of your own. Whether you go out for lunch every day or buy a new pair of shoes every couple of weeks, the first thing you need to do is sit down and figure out how you can reduce or eliminate those spending leaks to secure a more promising future for yourself. Retirement can be closer than you think.

Determine where your costs are. Where are you spending money that you do not necessarily have to?

LIVE BELOW YOUR MEANS

This should be a given, but considering the rising amount of consumer debt in America, it seems apparent that a huge portion of society is living above their means — that is, buying things that they might otherwise not be able to afford to buy without the help of credit cards and consumer lines of credit that might take years to repay. Many of these people often pass that debt on to their children.

An individual planning to retire early must avoid falling into this consumer spending trap. While credit can be a helpful and useful tool when buying necessary big-ticket items such as a home or a car, it becomes more of a burden when used to buy electronics, vacation's and other items that you do not need. To live below your means, you must not put anything on a credit card that you cannot pay off by the time the credit card statement arrives in your mailbox.

Before you buy something, consider whether or not the purchase will help you meet your goals. The ability to live below your means is characterized by knowing the difference between your needs and wants and using that information to help you make choices that will help you meet your future needs without feeling completely deprived. Try reconsidering your priorities and obligations to yourself and society. Are these priorities going to best serve you in your quest to retire early? Or are they hindering your progress in that area? Is it time to restructure the way you see the world and your financial relationship to it? If that is what it takes to achieve the financial freedom that will allow you to retire early, you need to consider your willingness to make those changes to better secure your future.

Credit is certainly a useful tool when it is managed effectively. It is important not to let those credit cards and accounts live for you, though.

So, take care of your needs first. Then, prioritize the things you want and begin to make choices that will not only make you happier and more fulfilled now, but in the future as well.

TAKE ADVANTAGE OF FREE MONEY

There is a good chance that your employer offers a pension, profit sharing plan, or other retirement benefit. If so, do not hesitate to contact your human resources professional to learn what that benefit can do for you. If such a benefit is offered, it is important to find out what your benefit is worth and when you will be eligible to receive it. These benefits are essentially free money for doing no more than the job you are already getting paid to do. The amount is calculated as a percentage of your annual wage and years of service to your company and invested by your company on your behalf, with or without further contribution from you.

It is more likely in today's market that your company offers a 401(k) or similar product. Income that you invest in your 401(k) comes out of your pre-tax pay. Therefore, you are able to save money on your tax bill while you invest in your future.

Furthermore, your employer might offer to match a portion of your contribution. The amount that an employer will invest on your behalf varies. But some employers will match 50 percent of your contribution, up to 6 percent of your salary. What this means is that they will invest $1 for every $2 that you contribute.

If your employer does not offer a retirement plan, consider opening an IRA and having deposits made from your checking account at regular intervals. The IRA contributions are tax deductible and will save tax dollars at the end of the year, enabling you to have more money to invest in your future.

It is important to understand that you should take advantage of any money that is offered to you for free to help you reach your target lump sum for early retirement.

It is important to identify as many ways as possible to add funding to your retirement. By starting as early as you can, plugging your spending leaks, and utilizing your financial resources wisely, you will be able to maximize the amount of money you have on hand for your retirement when you are ready to retire.

FACTS ABOUT TODAY'S MILLIONAIRES

Before exploring the things that you need to do to become a millionaire today, take into account what today's millionaires really are. You may be impressed and shocked.

- Did you know that today's millionaires are most likely earning an income of around $150,000 per year?

- Most are under age 60 and above age 45.

- Most live a comfortable but not over the top life. You would not know they were millionaires unless you saw their bank accounts.

- Most save 20 percent or more of the income they bring in.

- Most are married and have children.

- Many have not come from money but grew up in a poor family.

- Most have made their own money; they are self-made millionaires.

Do you fit into any of these categories or could you? By all means you can be a millionaire. Most millionaires are regular people, working standard jobs, raising their families, and spending and saving wisely.

The key thing to notice here is the fact that most millionaires are actually living a life style that is under their means, rather than over. This is essential if you plan to be able to retire early because you will need those funds to help you to retire.

Therefore, you have three simple goals to take into consideration at this point:

1. Always spend carefully, making smart spending decisions for the future.

2. Learn how to manage your money, which means learning how to invest it.

3. Be sure that you put away at least 30 percent of your income.

CASE STUDY: TED TOAL

For those just getting started with financially securing their future, the process starts with you, the consumer.

First, the person should take a look at their current expenses and put them down on paper. Then, they should imagine that they are retired today. They should picture in their mind what they see themselves doing, where they are living, and the activities they are doing on a daily basis.

Once they have a clear picture of retirement, they should go through their current spending per category and estimate what the expense will be in retirement using today's dollars. For instance, a person may want to travel more in retirement and want to increase this spending from a current $3,000 per year to $10,000 per year.

Fully understand the cost of healthcare and the expected inflation for these costs, which are much higher than average inflation. Especially if a person plans to retire prior to their eligibility for Medicare/Medigap, they will need to secure a private medical policy, assuming their former employer does not provide health coverage as a retirement benefit.

An experienced financial planner will be able to do many things that people can do for themselves but sometimes forget or simply overlook.

They will point out expenses that the person may have forgotten or underestimated. Again, healthcare costs are a big one. I have seen countless cases where people have put together retirement budgets and have completely forgotten to include any healthcare expenses or have drastically underestimated the expenses.

CASE STUDY: TED TOAL

They will also structure an investment portfolio based on annual inflation adjusted income needed. Retirement requires a much different investment philosophy today than in the past. Gone are the days when someone retired at 65 with a pension and social security and lived to 73. Today, individuals can expect to spend 20, 30, even 40 years retired. This will require a large amount of money! It is no longer appropriate to place all of your money into fixed income investments. A good financial planner can help structure a risk-controlled portfolio that can provide a steady stream of annual, inflation-adjusted income.

One situation that is often seen is this scenario: A person will ask, "I'm 50 and ready to retire. I haven't done anything before today to plan for this. Am I completely out of luck?"

My advice is this: Simply go through the steps mentioned earlier to determine your retirement spending need. Then, ensure that you have enough assets saved to provide an ongoing, inflation-adjusted income for these expenses while assuming a very conservative rate of return.

A financial planner will help you view the situation in real terms and provide a probability of achieving your goal. If the probability is less than expected, plans can be put into place to get you to the goal as quickly as possible.

Ted Toal
Toal & Associates, LLC
200 Harry S. Truman Parkway, Suite 110
Annapolis, MD 21401
410-224-0097
Fax: 410-224-0043

CHAPTER 8

GET YOUR PLAN TOGETHER

With a good understanding of where your money is coming from, it is time to put the pieces together. Developing your retirement plan means considering all aspects of what retirement for you, in particular, will be like.

The first thing to do is look at what retirement will be like in each stage of the game. Realize that retirement has different phases.

UP TO AGE 62

Life from the time you retire until you hit age 62 will be the most costly time of your early retirement years. The changes that happen now are most likely to effect what happens later. For most people, their children are grown up, done with school, and starting their own lives.

The first change will be health insurance. Since we have already covered this topic, this is just a reminder. Health insurance will be the largest factor because, without your employer providing it, you will need to do so.

Other changes may include your mortgage. The best course of action is to have your home paid off in full before retirement. A mortgage is a large monthly payment that will be hard to maintain after you retire, especially with the health insurance payment.

You should no longer need to worry about work expenses, such as the toll traveling back and forth takes on your car and clothing.

Take a look at your life insurance. The goal of life insurance is to care for those that are dependant on you. At this point, you do not need it. You may want to use it for your estate planning goals. Otherwise, you can cancel this expense. Another insurance product you do not need any longer is disability. Drop this as soon as you retire because you are no longer bringing in an income and nothing will be supplied to you.

Many people use these early retirement years to enjoy traveling, which is another large expense to take into consideration. To plan for this, choose a dollar value for the amount of traveling you would like to do per year. Adjust this later so that it fits your retirement goals as necessary.

Finally, you may take up more hobbies and activities now that you are not working. Therefore, it is essential to consider the added expense they may put on you and your family.

To determine what your costs will be for your first years of retirement, use the expense worksheet at the end of this book as a guide. Fill in the values for the costs of these expenses now and multiply them by the inflation rate. Total the columns to see how much you will need to have for that first year of retirement.

But what is your rate of inflation? Here is a quick chart to help you determine that.

YEARS UNTIL YOU RETIRE	INFLATION
10 Years	1.48
12 Years	1.6
14 Years	1.73
16 Years	1.87
18 Years	2.03
20 Years	2.1
22 Years	2.37
24 Years	2.56
26 Years	2.77
28 Years	3
30 Years	3.24

You will notice there is a line for filling in the cost of health insurance at the bottom of the expense worksheet. Your health insurance costs are going to be significant, but they will change during the course of your lifetime.

Estimates say that health insurance costs will rise as the rate of inflation rises. A good starting point, then, is to use this chart to help you with the cost of health insurance.

This chart is for one person, so if you are planning for a couple, double it.

YEARS UNTIL YOU RETIRE	COST
10	7,800
12	8,900
14	10,200
16	11,700
18	13,400
20	15,300
22	17,600
24	20,100
26	23,000
28	26,400
30	30,200

These numbers can be staggering, without a doubt, but they are one of the best tools to help you accurately plan for your health insurance costs.

FROM 62 TO 70

Now you are getting a bit older, and the cost of retirement is going to change. The biggest change during this time will be qualifying for Social Security and Medicare. Does that mean you can simply drop your health coverage? Most financial planners will tell you emphatically no.

Medicare is likely to undergo changes between now and the time you retire, and even if you do qualify and get full coverage, it does not always provide enough coverage and enough choices for most people. Your choices will be to secure your own insurance or to use a Medigap product as we discussed earlier.

What other changes will be happening in your life at this point? Perhaps not much will need to be tweaked at this point. You will need to adjust your health insurance, again using the inflation chart and health insurance costs to help you.

FROM 70 ON UP

Seventy years of age may seem like a big number and far away, but realize that you likely have another 20 years to go at this point. You should plan for at least another 25 years, though.

Now, you need to figure out your yearly costs. What has changed? You likely are not doing as much traveling at this time in your life. The largest concern here is your health. Could your health costs be rising? Perhaps you will need care beyond that which your spouse or family can provide.

When you complete the expense worksheet, use 4 percent as your inflation rate based on today's numbers. You want to be sure your health care also keeps up so use 7 percent per year. When all this is added up, you will have an estimated cost for your retirement years.

NOW A LOOK AT INCOME

Now have an idea of the costs you will incur during your retirement years. Where will the money come from to pay for those expenses?

Your income during retirement will depend on what your way of living is and becomes. For example, do you plan to work during these later years? Or will you live off the retirement investments you have put into place? Let us look closer at the income options you may have and find out where the money is going to come from.

In terms of your retirement income, most start out with a low amount, and until they reach the age of Social Security qualification, the amount will grow only slightly. If you work during retirement, your income will dip when you stop working. It will begin to rise when you are in yours 80s as your investments begin to kick in. However, when you get to be in your 90s your income may begin to drop because you will need extra funds to care for yourself.

SOCIAL SECURITY INCOME

Social Security will be the first consideration for income coming in after you retire (not including your investment benefits). When should you collect it? As discussed, the Social Security Administration has made significant changes as to when you can file for retirement, as well as how much you will qualify for.

A great place to find this information is the Social Security Administration. You can input your personal information and get a specific answer about your options. For example, include your age and information and find out how much you qualify for at this point in your life. Visit the Social Security Administration's Web site at **www.ssa.gov** to use these tools.

You need to think about the following things:

- When will you qualify for benefits, either partial or full? This number changes based on the year you were born. You may be able to start collecting partial benefits at the age of 62 and full at the age of 67.

- Should you collect Social Security early? You can do so, but if you plan to work after doing so, you will only be able to earn a maximum amount per year (currently this is $10,000 per year).

- When will your spouse qualify for Social Security? If planning together, the timing of when you will each qualify for Social Security should be considered. If you turn 62 but your spouse does not for another two years, that is two years you will not have those benefits.

For those that were born in 1960 or later, there are several ages at which you can retire to receive Social Security Benefits. At the age of 62 you can retire at the rate of 70 percent of full benefits. This amounts to $20,300 per year per person. Or you could wait until you were 67, when you can claim full benefits, which amounts to $29,000. If you retire between the ages of 62 and 67, your benefits will be between partial and full.

Many people do not believe they should collect early benefits but this can be misleading. For example, since you will be retired you may not need to collect on these funds until age 62, if you have planned well. Yet those years of collecting the reduced amount may give you an extra cushion even if you simply tuck it away to earn interest. You will receive it later, but it will take you over 11 years to make back what you could have received in those five early years.

CONSIDER THE INCOME THE FIRST YEARS

Where will you get the funds to manage the first years of your retirement? From the time that you claim Social Security on, you will have that benefit, pensions, and your retirement income from investment accounts to pay for your life style. But what about the money that will pay for the time between when you stop working and when you begin to receive Social Security?

Many people believe that they will simply withdraw from their retirement plans and use this money to fund these first years. The problem with that is that you will need that income to grow steadily so you can fund the later parts of your life. It should go untouched before you hit those last 30 years of your life.

The untaxable retirement accounts that you have should

be allowed to grow untouched because these will grow steadily over time without the threat of loss. For all your expenses of living from retirement until age 70, you should use taxable income accounts instead, if possible.

Here is an example: If you took out money from your 401(k) at age 50, you would face a hefty fee of about 10 percent as a penalty in addition to the tax that is levied on this money.

There are ways around this, some of which we will mention later. But the fact remains that these accounts are set up to manage your last years of life. By the time you are in your later retirement years, these funds should have at least doubled. Therefore, you should simply leave this money alone during early retirement.

OTHER INCOME SOURCES

There are other sources of income that have not been mentioned. For many, rental property or real estate investments will be a great way to help pay for early retirement. Ask yourself whether you will keep that real estate or sell it at the time of retirement. You should also consider how valuable that property will be then, not just now.

You may have outside sources of income that you are counting on. The rule of thumb is never to count on money unless you are 100 percent sure it will be yours to plan with. For example, you may be able to count on alimony, a trust fund income, or income from annuities.

Pensions should be looked at closely. At what age will you collect benefits and how much will they be?

What other forms of income are you planning to use to fund your retirement?

GET IT WRITTEN DOWN

SOURCE OF MONEY	YEARLY VALUE
Working Part Time	$
Spouse Income	$
Pension	$
Real Estate Income	$
	$
	$
	$
	$
	$
Total Income	$
Reduced By Tax (.90)	$
Net Income	$

What if you have nothing to include here? Chances are good that you are not really considering working part time, nor do you have this type of income coming in. That is fine. You will likely have no problem funding your retirement.

As you can see, we have yet to include your Social Security benefits here. Be sure to collect your benefits when you reach the correct age. Include this in the chart above, for you and your spouse.

Remember that although withdrawing your Social Security benefits early will ultimately reduce the amount of your benefits, it may be a source of funds to allow you to retire earlier than you could otherwise.

YOUR INCOME GOALS

What are your income goals?

- Determine what you will get from Social Security when you hit early retirement.

- Determine what income you will have coming in from other sources.

- Plan to have enough money in your taxable accounts that will fund your expenses until age 70 without touching your retirement accounts that are un-taxed.

The basis of the first part of this chapter was to give you an idea of what your expenses and incomes are and where it comes from. Now, we move on to generating the income that you need.

PULLING IT ALL TOGETHER

A simple plan for you to follow to determine how much you will need is this: Your income goals are reduced by your expenses. You want to have enough income to pay for your goals during your retirement years, but not so much money that you have to pay higher taxes and work longer to achieve this amount. It is a careful balancing act but one that you can do.

Now, unfortunately, it is not easy to balance the pieces out. Your life will change drastically at several times during your retirement. During your first years, you may still want to work part time. During that time, the extra income can pay for your needs and life style choices. But how is this made up during the time that you are no longer working?

We suggest that you plan to use your taxable income from the time you retire until age 70 when you will begin to use your retirement accounts (which are tax deferred accounts that are building your wealth over all this time). But, where will this taxable income come from?

Taxable income for the beginning years of your retirement (say from age 50 until age 70) will include income such as: pensions, investments, savings, Social Security, property rentals, and part-time work.

Tax differed income for the last years of your retirement (from 70 until at least 95) will include income such as: your employer sponsored retirement plan, your 401(k), and your IRAs. These funds are specific to this time in your life for several reasons. First, during the last years of your life, the compounding interest on these accounts will skyrocket their value. There will not be enough time for this to happen in the earlier parts of your retirement. Secondly, you will not have to touch this income until you are 70½ (for most retirement plans), and therefore you do not have to pay tax on them for all that time. Leave them there and plan to use only your taxable income for the first 20 years of your retirement.

HOW MUCH DO YOU NEED?

To understand how much money you need to have for your retirement in your taxable accounts as well as your tax deferred accounts, you must take several key factors into consideration.

Determine your expenses and income for your first years of retirement, from the age you plan to retire until you are 62 years old. Include all expenses and income that you plan to receive during this time. Your goal should be to have nearly all debts, including your mortgage, paid off by the time you hit 62. But also factor in the expense of health care.

Determine your expenses and income for your retirement from the age of 62 until you turn 70. During this time frame, you will have qualified for some level of Social Security (assuming that no changes are made until that time). When Social Security kicks in, you will be able to count on this extra income. You may lose some of your other income, however, and you may also qualify for Medicaid, which will help reduce your cost dependency on health insurance.

Determine your expenses and income for your retirement beyond the age of 70. At this point, you will have to begin pulling from your retirement accounts. Nearly all your retirement accounts (except for those in your Roth IRA) will require that you start taking distributions from them. That increases your yearly intake of money, but your expenses may begin to get larger because of expanding medical care needs.

Now, consider inflation. Inflation should be counted at least at 4 percent per year. Add this to each area of the worksheet. You want to understand as much as possible how much income you will need to have to pay for your expenses during each stage of the game. Remember, the 4 percent inflation not only comes into play with your expenses, but is factored into your income as well. Some situations will allow you more income as a cost of living increase, although this may be rare.

How much will your savings need to grow to reach your goals? In the strategies for retiring early that we have discussed here, you will find that our goal is that of 10 percent in growth on average each year. Some years will be more than others, though. The more money in both your taxable and your tax deferred accounts you have at the time you retire, the less worried you will have to be to meet your 10 percent goal.

Our savings strategy and investment strategies that are listed in the next chapters will help you create a situation that allows you to achieve this goal. You need to take into consideration what your specific needs are and then use our strategy to help you achieve that. Will you need to tuck away or invest $100 a month or a $1,000? That depends on where you stand in your income requirements for each segment of your retirement.

A key factor in this process is your willingness to work hard to make it happen. Most people will tell you honestly that it takes a long time to work through your goals and to develop a sound strategy. We are giving you an effective, simple, and easily doable strategy to gain the financial security you need. But you must put in the determination to make it happen. You will need to make early retirement your goal, and you must plan every decision around that.

HIRING PROFESSIONALS TO MAKE IT HAPPEN

Although we have stressed the importance of playing a role in your own future, there is no doubt that having a professional by your side will make the process of securing your dreams more achievable. Hiring professionals should be something that you do to create more details, more flexibility, and more legality to the process of retiring early. Can you do it alone? You can, but the added help of professionals will make your goals actually happen.

The first person to turn to for help is a professional financial planner. His job is to help you create an effective retirement plan. Note that you should always play a significant part in that planning, and it should be your ideas and plans that are used to make it happen, with the help of your financial planner's skills and knowledge.

Perhaps you have reached this chapter after quickly glancing through the last one. If the calculations and the details there seem to be too difficult, you are not alone. They are difficult and yet so important. With the help of a financial planner, this effect can be minimized considerably. More so, the financial planner will provide you with the details that you need.

WHAT IS A FINANCIAL PLANNER?

A financial planner is a valuable asset to those that are planning their retirement. When you identify what your personal goals are and define your financial goals, you can put the plan in motion. He or she will work through the process of making goals into reality.

The financial planner will help you in defining your net worth and creating the cash flow requirements. He can help you overcome virtually all aspects holding you back from your early retirement goals, too, by helping you determine the right solution and then making it happen.

The financial planner often is experienced in the process and also has the ability to use various computer programs to help define your goals. The software will define how much money you will need at various points when you retire, as well as how much you need to earn now to have those amounts saved.

There are various types of financial planners, all of which are good choices. Here are some that you can take advantage of. Realize, too, that the costs of hiring one or the other may be due to their level of experience. Carefully weigh costs with expertise.

RIA: A Registered Investment Advisor is a person that has registered with the Securities and Exchange Commission and markets themselves as an investment advisor or investment planner. This is a must for anyone that is looking for advice and plans to pay a commission for it. Sometimes a company called a brokerage will have agents working under the company's blanket RIA registration. Doing so is allowable.

CPA: A Certified Public Accountant is a person you may want to consider for this job, too. He or she is able to help with taxes, financial management, and much more. Many do not handle making decisions for you in terms of where to put your money, but will help manage the money and help make the most out of the tax breaks you can get.

CFP: A Certified Financial Planner is perhaps the most capable of helping you plan for your retirement. He or she provides a range of services, including helping to define your goals and crafting a comprehensive plan to make it happen. A Certified Financial Planner must be licensed and registered. He has to have at least three years of experience in the financial planning field before he can be licensed as a CFP. This helps give you the experience you are looking for.

THE FINANCIAL PLANNER'S JOB

The job of the financial planner that you hire will include

various things. His or her first task is to educate you. He will also help you by explaining the legalities that go into the process. He can help you understand the why's and how's. Most important, he must be patient, as you may have many questions.

In addition, he must work with you, not for you. He needs to listen to what you are looking for and what your overall goals are, not just what he wants you to create. A good financial planner is willing to sit down with you and give you advice, but he must be sure that your input is considered important.

Trusting your financial planner is a key aspect of hiring one. If for some reason you do not trust him or her, you will question and wonder about each aspect, decision, or determination that is made for you. You gain his trust by understanding the plan he offers to you and by knowing he has the experience it takes to make it successful.

It is just as important for the financial planner to be committed and working for you. You should know that you are not just a number in a file, but an actual person. You want to know that they are committed to helping you retire early step by step.

Yet, throughout the process, you should know that he is providing not just any advice but objectivity. You must know that he is offering you the best products and services for your goals, not for his own monetary benefit.

That is a tall order to fill, but when it comes to finding a financial planner, nothing else is acceptable. To find that perfect planner, start with a good idea of what you want him to do for you personally. Here are some tips to help you find the right financial planner for your goals.

INTERVIEW PROSPECTIVE FINANCIAL PLANNERS

Start with an interview. Ask questions about who he is and where he is coming from in terms of experience. What educational background does he have? Is he licensed and registered? Ask for references and check them out. You should also question what he would use to help you. Many will have a sample plan of what they have used for others and the likely outcome that they can show you. At this point, provide what information you feel comfortable with and no more. You are interviewing him for his qualifications of working with you, not the other way around.

CONSIDER HIS OR HER CONTRACTS

Next, determine what services he has to offer you. What products and services will fit your needs? Find out if the financial planner actually sells these financial products or simply manages them. You also want to know if he is representing any companies in particular (this is often a warning that he may push these companies over others that might be a better fit).

Find out about contracts and payments. How is the financial planner going to work with you? How often is he or she available? Will you pick up the phone and talk to him or to different people every time? The more you learn about the company and the person the better your decision can be.

REFERENCES AND REFERRALS

You may want to consider talking to family and friends about who they work with, as well as what types of good and bad histories they have had with people. If your cousin used a specific planner, what experience did she have with them, and if she is no longer using them, why not?

When it comes to references and referrals from your own family, be skeptical of hiring anyone you know directly and consider a family member or friend. You cannot assume that you can have a working, professional relationship if you do not commit to finding someone you are not affiliated with. If you hired Uncle Jim to be your financial planner, you would need to share all your financial details with him. If he does not do a good job, are you going to feel comfortable firing him? The best advice is to steer clear of hiring anyone with whom you have a personal relationship.

DO YOUR HOMEWORK

By doing your homework, you will be able to determine if the financial planner you are considering is the best for the job. Check out the financial planner through the licenses and registrations that he holds. There are some organizations that can help you, too. Here are a few resources for you to use:

ORGANIZATIONS TO HELP CHECK YOUR FINANCIAL PLANNER	
The Certified Financial Planner Board of Standards	888-CFP-MARK **www.cfp-board.org**
National Fraud Exchange	800-822-0416 (For background checks)
North American Securities Administration Association	202-737-0900 **www.nasaa.org**

Once you have gathered all this information, make a decision on the right financial planner for your needs. You should feel comfortable with the person you are working with. He or she should have the best qualifications and clearly define what he will do for you. You should be able to talk with him easily, and he will be able to have the knowledge and experience to help you. You should clearly define the costs of working with him, and be sure to take that into consideration when planning out your retirement goals. The balance of cost and experience, qualifications and communication is the best result for anyone looking for a financial planner.

With the help of a financial planner, as well as the plan you have developed, you will be well on your way to planning a successful early retirement.

GET A TEAM IN PLACE

You should realize that it may take some professional help

to make your early retirement happen. As you will see throughout this book, we recommend the help of various professionals. Your team should include:

- **A financial planner** that is dedicated to helping you achieve your goals. Your financial planner should have the ability to help with investments, to help you craft an effective savings plan, and to help you to pay down debt quickly. He should be able to advise you on investments, although you can hire another professional for this task.

- **A tax professional** has the job of helping you create an effective tax avoidance plan. As you will see, the cost of taxes on retirement plans can be heavy. If you do it right, though, you can avoid those taxes (legally of course) and minimize the pain in paying the IRS. A tax professional will help you minimize tax payments from the start.

- **An insurance professional** to help you with insurance investments from now until you retire. Some insurance products will not be necessary to have all your life. For that reason, you should invest in someone that will be honest and straightforward with you, not someone that is looking to sell you virtually every type of insurance product.

- **An attorney** that is dedicated to estate planning is also helpful. This person can help you make all your wishes happen legally. He also can help you avoid estate taxes later and help you structure your wishes so that they actually happen.

Together, this team of professionals will help you achieve all your goals. Do not worry about the cost of them. The money will come back to you in the long run when you can make the right decisions regarding all your investments and plans. We strongly suggest playing a role in each area, but having professional help is never a bad thing.

CHAPTER

9

THE RIGHT INVESTMENT STRATEGY FOR YOU

The process of winding up with enough money at the time you retire is not one that is simple and straightforward. It used to be simple enough: Put away at least 25 percent of your income into a decent earning savings account, and you would have enough to live on after your retirement happened.

That is no longer true because many do not want to put aside that much of their income, the costs of health care have skyrocketed, and people are living longer. The best way to wind up with enough money in your pocket is to make wise investment decisions and to allow the compound returns to do the work for you.

If the term investment worries you, step back and realize that it does not have to be that difficult. Investments do not have to be overly difficult to manage and they are not all as risky as you may believe they are. If you are someone that is comfortable with investments, you will be well on your way to using this information to help you put away enough money for early retirement. Even if you do not have this confidence just yet, you will.

Today, it is increasingly important to plan for your retirement as early as possible and to commit to long-term investments to make it happen. At this point, you should realize the importance of having an established 401(k) or other non-taxable plan in place. The importance of a 401(k), IRA, or Roth IRA is not in just how much you put into them, but how they compound over time. Whatever money you are placing in them at this point is going to compound for as long as 40 years. Even when you do break into this bank of money during retirement, the balance of it will continue to grow while you slowly pull money out to use.

WHERE DO YOU GO FROM THERE?

The process of investing in your future is a combined effort of more than just those plans. It should take into account low costs, low taxes, low maintenance (otherwise you may not take care of it well enough), and it should be something that provides you with safety over a long period of time. Stock market returns are a good example.

While stock market returns are the way to go, realize that nothing is ever guaranteed. Professionals will tell you that over a long period of time (anywhere from 30 to 50 years), you can invest up to 80 percent of your money into the stock markets and have confidence in it.

To accomplish this, several key elements must be used.

Here are the three that are the backbone of success in investing:

1. Money market mutual funds

2. Index funds

3. Bond mutual funds

INDEX FUNDS

In this strategy of investing, the core is in index mutual funds. You may have heard of these referred to as an S & P Index Fund. This fund represents 500 of the United States' very best companies. The reason why this is so crucial is in the return on investment. Over the last 75 years, this fund has shown an average of an 11 percent return. That is a considerably stable and highly valuable fund.

Still, look at this fund closer. You will find that over any ten year period, only 20 percent of stock mutual funds will beat the S & P funds, but there is no way to know which of those stock mutual funds will do that. More so, even those rare few that do beat the S & P fund will only do so by a fraction. This shows you just how valuable it is to invest in a solid S & P fund strategy like we recommend here.

Other options include the Wilshire 5000 Index and the Total Market Index Fund. The common bond between them is that they all work to invest in large cap companies. A market cap is the value of the shares of the company multiplied by the market price on a per share basis. You are investing in companies that offer the largest market cap.

An index fund is a group of stocks or bonds that are representing the stock market or a piece of the stock market. These work as a benchmark or a gauging point for where other funds are measured against them. The S & P, or Standard and Poor's, fund is the top 500 companies in the United States. The S & P does not in any way manage the funds in that grouping. There are many more groupings like this that are also index funds that can be selected. There is no managing of these funds, which helps to keep management costs low.

Part of this is the reason why you want to invest in index funds. For example, there are no management fees tied to index funds. There is a computer tracking system these companies use, and when there is an addition or change during the course of the year, the trade orders are automatically issued. There are few to no capital gains to be dealt with, mainly because there are so few sales. More so, there are no transaction costs to be dealt with.

The companies that are in this index fund determine the share price as a collective agreement. This percentage is done yearly, and when it happens to be time to sell your shares, you will have a capital gains tax applied to how much your share has increased over the time you have held it. Yet even this tax is much more affordable than other similar investments, and therefore makes this an affordable option.

BOND MUTUAL FUNDS

The next area to consider is that of bond mutual funds. This is what we call a fixed income investment. You may already have something similar, such as the CD at your local bank. You place money into the fund, and over a specific length of time it earns a specific percentage for you. You get your money back when the fund has fully matured. There are several types of these fixed income investments, including money market accounts, U.S. government securities, corporate debt securities, and bond mutual funds.

The U.S. government, corporate, and money market accounts are essentially a loan from you to the company. You loan your money to them for a specific time period and expect a return for doing so. The rate of interest charged is defined at the beginning of that time period. In a bond mutual fund, there is a collection of bonds of various types, including different types, different qualities, and different maturity dates. Each month, the managing company will take expenses from the account and add interest to it. In some instances, there is a capital gain dividend that is paid one or two times per year. This is done when the manager of the fund has made a profit on the sale of the fund.

The fund share will increase when your total value, which includes the value of the bonds, increases. This rate of value changes daily as they are revalued daily. You only benefit from these increases in value when you sell the shares you own. There is no maturity date, and therefore to get to your money you must sell your shares. When you do sell your shares, either to a capital gain or capital loss, you are selling at the current value of the share. When you reinvest the dividends monthly, you will purchase additional shares of the fund at the current valued share price.

A safe bet is the U.S. government bond fund because it invests in United States Treasury notes, which are guaranteed by the government. These pay more than other bonds that have a shorter maturity, but are in the middle range entirely. They generally have a maturity date within ten years, making them safe and less volatile.

MONEY MARKET MUTUAL FUNDS

Next, look at the third part of the puzzle for early retirement success. The money market mutual fund is the perfect addition, but you should realize that this is unlike the money market account that you may have at your local bank. This fund pays distributions from the net interest that is earned, and that rate is generally two times as much of the money market account at your local bank. There is no guarantee with this type of fund, but it is very rare for anyone to lose money in them either.

Most often, the distributions are about the same as the U.S. government fund. There are no capital gain dividends. Their price remains at $1 per share. Most funds have a 50 to 90 day average maturity. A manager will purchase new securities as older ones mature.

USING PORTFOLIO STRATEGIES AT YOUR AGE

Depending on where you are at, you will need to select the

right type of portfolio for your needs. Using the information about investments just given, we can break down where you stand into one of three categories. Determine which category fits your situation currently, but realize that this will change over time.

Building Wealth Portfolio

In this portfolio you are still working and still adding money to your investments, including your retirement plan. In this situation, your goal is to build your wealth. Both taxable and tax deferred options should be used. This gives you the largest return on your investment with the most safety. In this method you will put at least 80 percent of your money into the S & P Index Fund, and the other 20 percent should be in U.S. government bond funds.

This gives you 80 percent of your money earning 11 percent per year, as the other 20 percent earns 5.3 percent per year, or a total of 9.86 percent per year increase.

WEALTH MAINTAINING PORTFOLIO

In this portfolio the taxable accounts and the funds in your retirement accounts are included.

At the time of retirement, you will probably use your taxable investments to pay for your every day needs. By the time you hit age 70, you will likely need to withdraw funds from your retirement accounts. When this begins to happen, it is now time for you to change your portfolio a bit to match this new need. In this regard, you will have

70 percent of your portfolio invested in S & P Index Funds, while the other 30 percent is in government bond funds.

This gives you 70 percent of your money earning 11 percent per year and 30 percent of your money earning 5.3 percent every year, or a total of 9.29 percent per year.

When you make this change, you are making the portfolio more stable even though you are removing funds from it. More so, you are also protecting yourself from any large stock market decline.

Preserving Wealth Portfolio

The final option is that of preserving your wealth. This portfolio method allows you to manage your funds in late retirement, after you have turned 80. This will help stretch out your money safely, giving you as much as possible so that you do not outlive your money.

Having stability is the most important element because a stock market decline could severely hurt your remaining money. To do this, you create a portfolio that looks like this:

Thirty percent of your money remains in the S & P Index Fund while the other 70 percent of your money is in a bond fund. This gives you 30 percent of your money earning 11 percent every year while 70 percent of your money is earning 5.3 percent per year, or a total of 7.01 percent per year.

Revisions Are a Must

It would be easy to pick out a few stocks and investments and just let them work for you, assuming that they will always provide the best option no matter what stage of life you are in. Unfortunately, it is rarely that easy to make this happen. Instead, what you must do is revise and rebalance where you stand each year so that you can make the right adjustments for the coming years.

To start, you will need to adjust the amount you remove from your retirement accounts starting at age 70. You also need to determine the amount that you need to place into the money market fund for your taxable account. Finally, determine how many shares of the index fund you need to sell to maintain the 70 percent/30 percent that you need. In most years you will be able to take the money from selling the index funds and place it into the money market account.

When you take the time to do this each year, you are able to have at least three years of expenses not tied into the market. Therefore, you do not have to worry about stock market hits that may happen along the way. This also prevents you from having to sell shares from your funds that are dropping in value.

WHAT ABOUT THOSE TAX COSTS?

Taxes and retirement may seem like they go hand in hand, but in truth the three portfolio options we discussed are very low taxable accounts. These index funds do not pay out high dividends but rather pay out very little, meaning that you do not have to pay large amounts of taxes on them. The gains that are received are built up into the value of the share price. The bond fund and the money market fund dividends in your taxable accounts will pay taxes.

You will pay taxes when you sell off the shares of taxable account holdings that you have in index fund shares and when you take withdrawals from your retirement accounts. When you retire, you will sell index fund shares from your taxable account every year. Because you are likely to be in the lowest tax bracket, you will pay much less. The sale of these shares are long-term capital gains and therefore are taxed at a fraction of what other gains are taxed.

You also have the other two types of funds, including bond and money market funds. These are taxed a bit higher, currently 15 percent. Yet you still must consider that you will be able to shelter much of this income from taxes because of standard deductions and exemptions you likely qualify for.

What does all this mean? It means that when it comes time to withdraw from your accounts to pay for your retirement, if you follow the portfolios listed here, you will face low cost taxes and will build money to use during retirement safely yet steadily.

Index funds offer you an ideal way to invest without the risk of other methods, but also provide you with a range of low cost securities that can help you to avoid many of the pitfalls of retirement income.

For those still leery about investing and the tax situation, there are professionals that can help you. Hiring a professional financial planner is the first step, and if you are confused about the taxes, hire a tax professional to guide you through the process. They can make recommendations to help you get the most from your money.

MAKING INVESTING SECOND NATURE

Perhaps the essential element in the process of retiring early is to make investing and saving second nature. It is easy to push off the savings for a month here or a month there because something else becomes important. But doing so will cost you considerably. You must make it a habit to save and then spend second, only after your savings and investing have taken place.

Remember that what you invest now and what you make from that investment is what will pay for up to half of your adult life. It is what is going to allow you to retire early. To make the process as simple as you can, be sure to plan according to the time and energies you have. For example, while you are younger and busy with life, make your investment plan as simple as you can, even allowing it to run on autopilot. When you do retire, you will have more time to enjoy the learning process that comes along with investing in the stock market.

SAVE AGGRESSIVELY

To invest money, you must have the money to invest. For this to happen, you have to be aggressive in the savings you do. To save, you must meet various goals, including these:

- You should have paid off all the debt you have except for your mortgage, a car loan, and perhaps some school loans.

- You must have at least three to six months of emergency funds tucked away someplace, preferably in an account that is easy to access, earning some interest but far enough away that you will not use it for non emergencies.

- You must have quality health insurance that protects you (and your family) from most high cost situations.

- You must have insurance products to cover yourself and your family, including a homeowner's or home renter's insurance policy, life insurance (while you are earning money from employment), and disability insurance for both you and your spouse while you are working.

Once these goals are met, you can begin working on savings. How aggressive is aggressive enough? You should aim for at least 25 percent of your income. This is aggressively saving, and it will pay off.

Let us say that you save $400 a month. If this is 25 percent of your income, you will find it to be an ideal amount to put away. After a few years, it will grow considerably. When you put away a steady stream of income every month (and then invest it wisely) you will make a solid amount of income from it. That $400 per month becomes much more in the long run.

When you are an aggressive saver, putting money away each month is hard but not nearly as difficult as trying to make it up by being an aggressive investor. You can control the amount of money you put into savings for investing. But you cannot control the markets, and it can be a risky situation when you are betting your retirement on investing aggressively when you have not saved enough. Many people feel that they must invest aggressively to make enough to retire early because they have not saved enough or have not started soon enough. You can avoid this.

TAX AND INFLATION CAN HURT

Taxes and inflation will cut into your profit margin, but strategies can help you make it as painful as possible.

You may want to complain about taxes, but you should realize that the government is allowing you to keep most of the taxes in your retirement accounts for a fairly long time (until you withdraw the funds). This means that, during that time, the tax cost to you is allowed to compound over time and build more wealth. In other words, taxes may be brutal, but they are working in your favor.

You will be taxed on the income that you make from your investments. This comes in the way of capital gains, interest payments, and dividends in your taxable accounts.

Can you avoid taxes at all? While it is illegal not to pay your taxes, you can avoid them for as long as possible, allowing your money to build wealth through compound interest. To make this happen, you need to invest in mutual funds that offer a low turnover of stocks and that means virtually no capital gains are shown as dividends. Because of these long-term holding options discussed here, you will not have to pay taxes for a fairly long time. When the shares of these stocks are sold, you will need to pay taxes, but until then, the funds are compounding.

What about inflation? Inflation is yet another undeniably frustrating but unavoidable fact that you must face. You cannot avoid it, but you can invest wisely to overcome it. Your goal is to invest money in such a way that it grows quickly and faster than the rate of inflation, after taxes are deducted from it. To do this, you need to aim for a 3 percent above inflation goal in the growth of your investments. While on a yearly basis you may see more or less growth, it will balance out to be enough in the long term to beat out inflation's toll on your investment money.

REALIZE YOUR GOAL IS LONG TERM

As you begin to dabble in the stock market, you must be aware of what your role in that market is. Realize that you are a long-term investor, looking to make money over the long haul. You are not looking for short spikes in the market that you can benefit from. By being a long-term investor, you gain the ability to be more conservative and safe while still earning a solid return. You also have the ability to withstand the ups and downs of the market.

It is said that, for every year that the market is down,

there are three more years when the market is up. For that reason, being a long-term investor allows you much more room to make decisions and to realize your goals. It is less important that you have a high percentage growth each year.

You must also take the time to learn what type of investor you are. Each person is going to be different when it comes to investing in the market. Some will make more money than others, but remember that there is not one way to make money. You are different from the next guy that is investing in several ways. Your needs and desires may vary. You have long-term goals, whereas the next guy may have short-term goals. More so, the type of investing personality you have will cause a different outcome, too. The bottom line is that, even though you may be different from other investors, you can succeed at your investing goals.

The key factor in any investment strategy (especially the long-term goal) is compound interest. This is when your return will continue to make more returns for you in the future. Your profit is put right back into the investment so that you can earn interest on that, too. Aggressive saving can help you see compound growth happen over and over again, which is what truly triggers a massive investment well worth your time.

Do not make the mistake of being afraid to invest in the stock market. Some people are worrisome about doing so because of the risk there is to losing money. As mentioned, you will only lose money in the stock market when prices drop and you sell off those shares. You should not have to do this and therefore you should not lose nearly enough money to worry about. Those that are afraid of the stock market, especially during a dip in the market, are likely to try and pull out, but this can be the biggest mistake. Instead, if you let your money ride out the storms in the stock market, chances are good that you will still profit.

The other troublesome thing that happens to many investors is greed. Those that find themselves in a good situation in which there is the potential for a good return may find this to be the time to begin aggressively investing. They may plug more and more money into their portfolio because it is doing so well. But be careful. Changing your course can cause you to face an abrupt market change, which can cost you considerably.

The key is to be balanced in your investing. Do not be overly greedy, but do not be so conservative that you pull out at the slightest dip. You must find a way to deliver the highest quality returns for your retirement plan, not just immediate gratification.

What does it take to be a successful investor? Many things, including being able to enjoy this method of building wealth for your future. You should know what you can do and what your goals are. Never push for too much, too fast. With the plan outlined here for you, you are well on your way to finding a comfortable position in the stock market. Be sure that you are employing the help of professionals that can offer advice, as well as management of your accounts for you. Doing so makes the process of investing that much more successful.

CASE STUDY: WILLIAM RASHKE

When asked why he planned his retirement early, Mr. Rashke's answer says it all: "I wanted to retire early to start enjoying life early, as you never know what is down the road. I wanted to do more traveling and just things that I wanted to do, such as hunting, fishing, and doing yard work at my own leisure."

Finding the right amount of money to put away for retirement is the key to being successful when you are retired. To do that, he says, "You have to look at your assets, such as the amount of your retirement plan or 401(k), whichever it may be, or stocks, mutual funds, CDs, and so forth. You now need to look at the expenses you currently have, such as the mortgage, college funds for your family, and what it costs you to live on a monthly basis. Then, consider the rising cost of living into the future. After weighing all these factors, then you make a decision. You have to ask, 'Can I do this financially?'"

"There are times when you think, 'Did I do the right thing?' and I do think everyone goes through that. You can always go back to work part time to interact with people again or take classes or join organizations or even volunteer somewhere."

When asked about making the right decisions to get to retirement, Mr. Rashke says, "If I felt I could buy a larger home or go on a nice vacation, I would, but I would also make sure I had the cushion behind me for any unforeseen things that could happen. You also need to look at what your Social Security will be, if you can take it early or wait until you reach that age. I would suggest taking it early, even if it is a smaller amount to fund some of these needs."

William Rashke
Retiree
Broadview Heights, Ohio

CHAPTER

10

THE TRUE SECRETS
TO INVESTING

Avariety of people are in the stock market today making solid money. Each one has their own strategy for success. Being unique can work for you, or you can try and follow a preset strategy, too. The ultimate must is to have a strategy and to follow it as closely as possible.

If you wish to be successful in the stock market, you must have a strategy to use. That is a secret that any successful investor has. Without a strategy, you will make many mistakes throughout the time you are investing. For example, you may come upon a situation in which you have to determine what decision to make based on what you think is going to happen in the market. Or you may make decisions based on the way you feel today or what the latest news is. None of these decisions are going to deliver the long-term steady return on your investment that you need.

So, what strategy should you develop? That is up to you,

but here are several of the key elements that should play a role in the strategy you use.

MAKE YOUR MONEY WORK

The first place to start is to always keep your money working for you. You may have heard the term "lazy money" used to describe money that is not earning enough interest. For example, your bank account or money market account is earning some interest, but it could be earning much more (even two or three times as much) if the money was invested in the stock market correctly.

Now, that is not to say that all your money should be in the stock market. In fact, your emergency funds, living expenses, and other short-term accounts should not be. But any money that is not serving its purpose to the fullest extent should be working to earn you as much money as possible.

If you plan to retire early, at least 80 percent of your non-short-term savings/emergency accounts should be invested in the stock market.

If you wish to make this amount of money work for you, you have to know what to do with it to make that happen. You will have to accomplish all these goals to make that happen:

- Develop a basic investment strategy that works for you and that you are comfortable using.

- Determine how and when to invest the money to fit your strategy.

- Make changes when it is necessary to meet the goals of your portfolio and your strategy.

Some of this work can be done by the professionals that you hire. But you must make decisions yourself on how to manage these funds correctly. They cannot do everything for you.

KEEP PUTTING MONEY IN

You must continue to put money into your investing accounts if you are to be successful in growing your portfolio. Every pay period or every month, money needs to be saved so that you can reach the goals you set for yourself. This process is essential as it helps to build your portfolio fast.

The process is called dollar cost averaging. In this method you are investing the same amount of money at regular intervals, no matter what the price is at. When you do this, you purchase more shares at the lowest prices and buy less at higher prices. This gives you an average cost that is lower than the average price over the long haul.

If you somehow come into a large chunk of money, what should you do with it? As long as the money is getting put away for at least five years, put it all in at once, without worrying about the dollar cost averaging method. A lump sum of money at one time is going to give you better returns even after just a few years.

ASSET ALLOCATION AND DIVERSIFICATION

Two additional considerations are asset allocation and diversification. We have discussed both of these already so we will only touch on them slightly here. As part of your portfolio, these elements are incredibly important. Asset allocation is spreading your money around and placing it in different types of investments. This means that you can select the best locations but not put all your money into the same place.

Having a variety of options in your investments gives your portfolio some security because it provides protection from the short-term ups and downs of the stock market. This does slow down the growth of your portfolio to some degree. If you placed all your money into one type of investment and that investment went through the roof, you would no doubt make more money if you had more of your money in that investment rather than lesser producing investments. At the same time, though, you need to consider the risk factor.

With that comes diversification. Here, you want to spread your money around inside the investments you have. If you put all your money into one company and that company bottomed out, you would find yourself struggling to make ends meet. But when you invest your money in several different companies, this risk is reduced, and the end result is that it gives you more protection.

KEEP THE PROCESS SIMPLE

Invest in any way that fits your style and your abilities,

but always be sure that the process is simple. The more complex the strategy and the details are, the more difficult it will be for you to pull it all together for success. Micro management is not going to be right for everyone in planning out their portfolio.

To keep it simple, choose and then stick with your strategy, whatever that is, until you are satisfied. You must realize that the long-term goals are the most important, not the short bursts that may cause the value of your shares to drop some here and there. You also need to buy your stock with the purpose of holding it long term, which means that you should not be able to talk yourself into purchasing stock that seems to be "hot" at the moment. Rather, always pursue long-term goals with the stock instead.

You should not need to over-allocate your options or over-diversify. If you have to do this, it becomes more work, which may mean that it will not get done correctly or as often as you would like it to. The more complicated the picture and practice is for you, the less likely you will be to find the time or the energy to put things in place. On the other hand, if you invest in a strategy that is simple and straightforward, you can count on being able to fully manage the portfolio in a matter of minutes.

When you have a large variety of managed mutual funds, you may see yourself as having benefits, but you also have additional costs to consider. Managed fund fees can be quite costly, anywhere from three to ten times as much as the costs for managing your S & P Index Fund. The problem is that these fees come out of your profit margin, making it more difficult for you to make the funds you need. In addition, you may also have to deal with a high turnover of stocks each year. This means that you will end up with capital gain dividends, which lead to paying taxes on your taxable accounts. All this amounts to a costly experience.

Instead, your goals should be very simple. Do your best to find and invest in a strategy that is low cost to run and offers no high expenses. Be sure that your strategy takes into account the best way to grow your investments while deferring taxes as long as possible. Avoid looking for the next big stock break or chasing after the company that did outstanding last month. Concentrate your efforts on looking for steady, stable returns.

Also, keep in mind that your money and your portfolio are yours alone to manage even if you do hire people to help you manage them. It is ultimately up to you to make decisions regarding the process. A route that offers simplicity and flexibility will likely be the best way to go.

SO YOU WANT TO MANAGE YOUR OWN MONEY?

As the manager of your portfolio there are many ingredients that will gain the most growth for you and provide you with the payoff of early retirement. Remember that no one out there cares as much about the success of your portfolio as you do, not even the financial planner being paid for the performance of your portfolio.

HOW WILL YOU CHOOSE TO MANAGE YOUR PORTFOLIO?

The answer to that question depends on many other factors, including:

- The amount of time you have for researching, reading, and learning about each investment, the risks involved with it, the current market conditions, the industries you may invest in, and the companies themselves.

- You also need to determine how willing you are to commit the time to doing just that. If you do not enjoy this type of research, chances are you will not do the research as well as it needs to be done.

- Are you confident in your ability to make the right investment decisions? And when things begin to change, do you feel you are confident enough to make the right decision for selling at a loss or at a gain? If you make a mistake, will you be able to accept that mistake?

You must be willing to learn how to do anything listed above that you do not know how to do. Some people do not put in all this work, and they go off whims and guesses about the market. This is anything but the right way to manage your portfolio. Instead, dedicating time and work to executing the plan that you create is the best way of making it all come together.

The plan that we offer as an example is one that uses the

S & P Index Fund, as well as a money market mutual fund and the U.S. Treasury bond fund. This plan will work for you because it has been tested over the long haul, and it is low cost, effective, and has low taxes. It is not, however, the only option you have.

Only you can determine if this is the right decision to make. You may also want to use this plan and then add additional investment opportunities to it. That is a great decision, and when done well it will help you make more of a profit.

Your goal should be to see the same or better results in the growth of your portfolio as the S & P Index Fund will see. If it beats or matches the S & P at least three out of five years, you are doing well. It is rare to make this happen every year, even if you use experienced fund managers.

What if you are unsure about making this type of decision? The best recommendation for you at this point is to dedicate your time to using the method we have outlined with the S & P Index and use it as a window into the stock market. You will learn about the various options out there and how the market works. Then, you can test the waters slowly and learn through experience. Ultimately, experience will be the best teacher.

INDEXES WORK FOR YOU

A good place to get started in managing your own portfolio is to understand the indexes out there. In short, an index is a way of dividing up the stock market into segments. To measure your portfolio's performance, you need to have a benchmark, or a source to compare your portfolio to. When you do this, you can see how much your portfolio grew compared to how these indexes have done.

There are several very popular indexes that are continuously used by most fund mangers to help with measuring success. The S & P Index is one of them. This measures some 499 (plus Nestle) companies that are considered large cap companies in the United States. Other options include the Russell 1000 (1,000 largest U.S. Companies) and the Russell 2000 (the next 2,000 companies). You also can use the Wilshire 5000, which is all New York Stock Exchange and national Association of Securities Dealers and Automated Quotation (NASDAQ) stocks.

There are hundreds of other indexes, and you can use any of them. Check the Web for more options or using the Wall Street Journal (which offers another 20 indexes that can be used and are tracked daily). The good news is that you do not need to have or use all these indexes to fully be successful with your portfolio. In fact, what you need to do is to only use a handful of them to diversify. Nevertheless, it can be nice to know what is out there and what options you have in each portfolio.

SECTOR FUNDS

Another area to explore is sector funds. These are funds that are linked together by the sector of the economy that they represent. For example, you will find transportation, multimedia, retail, and insurance being large sectors in which you can invest. When you invest in a sector fund, you are simply putting some of your money into the companies in a specific sector. The companies that are related to that particular business or industry are lumped together like this.

You should not put more than 10 percent of your portfolio in one sector. This is especially true if you have 50 percent or more of your investment in the S & P Index. The reasoning is quite simply because many of these sectors are already represented in the S & P Index, which means you have overlapping coverage. The most important sectors to avoid putting a large portion of your money in include financial services, pharmaceuticals, oil and gas, and telecommunications.

You should also avoid putting too much of your portfolio into the same sector in which you are currently working. For example, if you are getting company stock from your health care profession, you are also getting a paycheck from them and investing in health care in your portfolio. This is simply too much for one sector. A problem in that sector could do serious damage to your portfolio. Instead, you should try to keep a more balanced portfolio.

The best sectors in terms of performance include tobacco, banks, and utilities. These top performers have been in this position for between five and 15 years. Should you believe that they will continue to remain in that position, you should invest in them again. The most troublesome in terms of volatility are the sectors of technology, biotech, and health care as they see the most fluctuations. In addition, they also pay significant capital gains dividends, which translates into more taxes for you to pay and less profit.

For those that are interested in sector funds, be sure to look at the total picture. Adding some sector funds into your portfolio can be a great choice, especially as they can help to increase the total value of your portfolio over time. Avoid investing more than 10 percent of your portfolio's equity into one sector, though.

ADDITIONAL MANAGED FUND OPTIONS

If you are considering domestic equity mutual funds, world equity funds, or fixed income funds for your portfolio, select wisely. There are thousands of these to select from, all of which can offer you the options you are after if selected appropriately. A good way to see your options is to visit **www.morningstar.com**, which will provide you with more information on these classifications. There, you will see that the companies are grouped together based on their last known holdings and their recent performance. Although not exactly accurate, it gives you options to select from.

If and when you consider general equity funds like these, be sure to follow a few specific considerations. Do not go with more than six funds at one time, including any foreign or global funds. You also should be looking at the style box (see Morningstar for more information), as this will give you a clear path without overlapping too much coverage from stocks ownership. You should look for low fees and low turnover, as these do much better in the long run because you pocket more of the profit. You also want to plan on holding on to these funds for the long haul unless they are not performing well.

STOCKS

Perhaps you want to dabble in stocks directly. By all means, go right ahead. While you do not want to invest in 20 to 40 different companies, you may invest in just a handful of well-selected companies instead. These should be from a range of different industries to give you the most diversification in your portfolio.

For example, buying stocks means more work on your part. You will need to take the time to read through information on the stocks and do your homework on the market. You need to educate yourself on the stocks in various ways, including through financial reports, trade publications, brokerage analyst, research reports, and your own research.

There are various Web sites that can offer help to you, as well as various informational packages that you can request from the company itself (request an investor information package be sent to you). There is no limit to the amount of information you should be looking for. The more information you can gain, the better chance you will have of selecting the right stocks for your portfolio. Most important, you want to answer these questions:

- What does the company do and do so much better than their competitors?

- What is the company expected to do over the next year or two?

- Is the industry in which the company is in expected to grow? By how much?

- Do you support the company's plans for growth?

- How is management managing the company? Stability here is a must.

Learn what the company looks like on paper, too. You want to see the company's financial statements from the balance sheet to the profit and loss statement to the cash flow statements. Looking at these provides you with a solid understanding of the company's current situation and where they are heading in the near and long-term future.

What happens when you do buy stocks? You should realize that you should plan to hold on to them for at least three years. This gives the company enough time to actually put their plans into motion and to see results. Anything shorter is not a fair stake on your part. Unless there is some particularly bad news for the company, hold on to the stocks and see what happens after three years time.

Why should you sell? In most situations, it will not offer you any profit to sell your stock in a company unless they are not meeting your overall goals. If they are executing their plan accurately and seeing growth in profits, then by all means stick with the same stocks. Or if you find that they are far too ahead of the game and you are afraid they may drop back some, this too can be a sign for you to pull out.

Managing your own portfolio can be a challenge, but for those that fall in love with managing their money, it can be a lot of fun. The challenge can be motivating yourself to do it. If you have the ability and the time, we recommend starting slow but going for it.

RETIREMENT BUILDING WITHOUT THE TAX MAN

I n the last chapters we have discussed a number of factors that play a significant role in building your wealth, including investment strategies. Yet the most important factor in securing the wealth you need to retire early should come from your very own tax deferred retirement plans. Although we have mentioned these earlier, it is now that we will go into detail about just how important these retirement plans are for your success.

With some retirement accounts, like those discussed here, you can put away money every paycheck and allow it to grow and grow. Compounding happens here readily, giving you an increased ability to fund your retirement faster. In addition, you do not have to pay any taxes on these plans until you use the money. That is a good thing because, since you do not have to pay taxes for all that time, you are building wealth through compound interest even on the funds that are for tax purposes. For example, if you have $10,000 in your account, you are supposed to pay $1,000 in taxes on that money yearly. Because you do not have to pay this until you withdraw the money, the $1,000 remains, giving you $11,000 to build interest on. This small difference can amount to tens of thousands of extra dollars in your retirement plan.

There are a number of different accounts that this can be done with, but only specific accounts get this privilege. These types of accounts are set up through your employer or other means, but are specific to government regulations that govern them. Do not assume that there are no limits or no restrictions on paying taxes unless you are sure of it.

Some of the most common of these accounts include 401(k) accounts if you work for private companies or 403(b) or 457 accounts if you work for government agencies or public services. Some other choices include SEP-IRAs, Keogh plans, and SIMPLE IRAs, which we will define in just a bit.

Most of these accounts work in such a way that you and your employer can make contributions to them while you work for the company. It is extremely important for you to find out if your employer offers this type of retirement plan, and if so, how you can get involved with it. In many cases, this will be the backbone of your retirement income and savings, which means starting as early as possible is a must.

Remember that the funds you put into your retirement accounts are able to grow without being assessed taxes until later when you are at age 70 or even beyond. This is money that will work hard for you from day one.

401(K) RETIREMENT ACCOUNTS

The most common retirement account that is set up to be paid as described thus far is the 401(k) account. This plan is one that you will likely have offered to you by your employer. Over 40 million people working today in the United States are using a 401(k) plan for their retirement planning and savings.

This plan is called a defined contribution plan, which means they allow you to contribute a set amount of money per year into your account through payroll deductions. These plans are set up by your employer (if he does not offer one, ask why not). You can determine how much of your income from each paycheck you would like deposited into your retirement account through this automatic method. In many cases, employers can also contribute to the plan, giving you even more opportunity to save (and giving you free money to take advantage of).

Another benefit of your 401(k) plan is that it is portable. This means that you can take the account with you when you change employers, should you decide to (although there are restrictions on doing so).

Your 401(k) is still an account that you can control to some level. These are called self-directed plans because you can select which investments you would like your funds to be put into. You can choose from the options that are provided by the company managing the funds and the choices that your employer makes. These accounts give you the ability to put funds away for retirement. They will be invested as you see fit and are tax deferred until you withdraw the funds (which should not be for many years into your retirement if you use the plan put forth here).

In most cases, you do not have the ability to access these funds until you reach the age of 59½. If you do pull funds out of the 401(k) before this time, you will face not only the taxes but also a 10 percent penalty tax, which was put into place by the IRS, on the funds removed.

You may be wondering why you should put money any here else when you have such an ideal opportunity in the 401(k) plan. The fact is that there are limits to how much you can put into your 401(k) per year before you are taxed for doing so.

As of 2007, you can put up to $15,500 into your 401(k) yearly without any recourse from the IRS. This amount changes each year due to a cost of living adjustment, but generally goes up in $500 increments. In addition to this limit, there may be a limit to how much you can put into your retirement account as per your employer's plan. This information should be provided to you before you open your account or you can contract your human resource manager for more information.

If you are over the age of 50 and are trying to play "catch up" with your retirement plan, you can do this with an increased allowed amount. This number also changes each year, but currently that amount is $5,000 per year in addition to the $15,000 that you can put in.

The IRS also allows your employer to add funds to your 401(k) account as well. Your employer can put up to 6 percent of your pre-tax compensation into your 401(k) account as well. This number also changes per year depending on the cost of living increase given by the IRS.

Employers often match up to a certain amount for your retirement plan. If you put in nothing, they put in nothing. A common situation is for you to put in 3 percent of your income, and the employer will match at another 3 percent. This gives you a dollar for dollar match of the funds you put into your retirement account. It is very important to find out what type of matching option your employer offers and to maximize that.

For example, increase your investment to the highest amount possible so that you can pull as much as you can from your employer's investment. Be sure to increase your investment as high as possible so that you can enjoy the benefits that your employer is offering.

There are some regulations on these plans that you should know about. For example, your state may regulate when a 401(k) plan can be offered to an employee (such as at the time of being hired or after a year's worth of employment). They also may have other restrictions that should be noted.

WITHDRAWING FROM YOUR 401K FOR A NEW JOB

What happens when you leave your job? You will not want to leave your 401(k) at your previous employer for too long. The options you have are many, but not all should be used, and we will explain why.

You have three options. You can do nothing, and the money will stay with your current 401(k) account and continue to grow until you hit the age of 70½, at which time you are required to begin withdrawing the funds. You can do this if you have more than $5,000 in the account.

You can also roll over the funds to a rollover IRA. Or you can transfer the funds from the old employer's account to the next employer's retirement plan, assuming that the new employer's plan allows for transfers like this.

If you plan to transfer the money, you need to do so within the first 60 days of leaving, and it should be done between the plan trustees. If you do the moving of the money yourself, your employer is required to withdraw 20 percent of the funds for the IRS. You will have to replace this 20 percent. It is considered regular payroll withholding, and you will need to pay taxes using this money on your Form 1040 at the end of the year. Should you select not to replace the 20 percent that was removed, this is considered a taxable distribution, which opens the door for additional taxes, as well as a 10 percent penalty for withdrawing from the account before you hit 59½ years old.

If the funds do not rollover within the required 60 days, you will owe regular taxes on the funds that you receive, as well as the 20 percent that was taken by your employer. On top of that you will pay an additional 10 percent penalty tax for removing funds before you were 59½. This is factored based on the entire amount that is not replaced in the new account within those 60 days. All this will heavily tax the funds that you have.

Perhaps the best option for you when you are leaving your employer for a new one is to use an IRA. We will go into more detail about them in just a bit, but for now realize that they are an ideal tool for any retirement plan. If you roll over the 401(k) into an IRA, you will have the most flexibility in your move. You can select the financial institution that provides the rollover IRA on your own. Doing so gives you custodian control over the account. The best method of managing this rollover 401(k) is to take advantage of a large financial firm, such as Charles Schwab or Fidelity Investments. This will allow you to have many options in buying stocks and mutual funds and therefore gives you more control over managing your money than any other method.

If you wish to, and it is offered, you may be able to roll over your 401(k) into your new employer's retirement plan. Doing so can be difficult for several reasons. For some employer's plans, there is a minimum time that you must be working for the company before you qualify for the retirement account at all. If this is the case, you can put your money into an IRA until you qualify for the retirement account. If this is the route you take, be sure that the IRA is created solely for the funds from your retirement and does not have funds from other accounts added to it, or it could be near impossible for you to separate them to place it into the new account.

Finally, you could leave the funds in your pocket and forget about investing it. This is perhaps the worst decision you can make. All the taxes will hurt you, including:

- The 20 percent that your employer must take right off the top for withholdings

- The tax penalty of up to 10 percent of the value of the account that you will pay

- The standard taxes that apply to the money

If you are in the 28th percent federal tax bracket and have state taxes to deal with, too, all these costs can amount to more than 40 percent of the value of your account. You will lose nearly half the money that you have invested in.

That is only made worse when you consider the details. Let us say that you have $5,000 in your retirement account and want to pocket it instead of putting it into a new account. You will walk away with about $2,750 in your pocket once all taxes are paid. If you had left it in an account making 10 percent interest for the next 30 years and you never added any additional money to it, you would have had $115,000 in that account!

IT IS TIME TO RETIRE

Now it is time to retire. What happens with your 401(k) account? When you retire and leave your job at the age of 55 or any time thereafter, you are able to begin withdrawing funds from your 401(k) account. During this time you are not subject to the 10 percent pre-withdrawal penalty as long as you have stopped working. You will have to begin to pay regular taxes on the funds in the account at this time, though, as taxes will need to be paid at some point. You may be tempted to annuitize the money here. We strongly recommend not doing this because your money is unable to grow if you go that route.

If you do not want to leave your money in the current plan, you can use a direct custodian to custodian rollover IRA. Doing so would allow you to manage the funds on your own. That could be a good decision if you are able to manage your funds correctly.

Another option is to leave the money in the current plan or to roll it over into an IRA and leave it there until you hit age 70. If you do this, the funds will continue to grow and make you additional money. If you are able to secure a 10 percent return on these funds, you will find that the money will triple within 12 years and quadruple in just 15 years. These funds will help you pay for your expenses at the time of your retirement.

When you hit age 70½, it will become mandatory that you begin distributions from your 401(k) account. This is taxed as regular income. If you are still working at this age, you can leave the funds in your account until you retire before having to begin distributions of the funds.

Inheriting 401(k) Accounts

As part of the process of setting up a 401(k) account, you will need to select who will inherit the funds from this account should you perish. The beneficiary that you list is up to you, but it usually is your spouse.

If you are the beneficiary to your spouse's account and they perish, you have several options to consider in terms of what to do with these funds. You can leave the funds in your spouse's name, or you can roll the funds into an IRA with you listed as the beneficiary of the account and your spouse named as the owner of the account.

When you leave the funds in the spouse's name, you are able to withdraw and use these funds as you need to even before age 59½ without any pre-withdrawal tax penalties, although you will still need to pay taxes on the money. You may want to consider this because it gives you more access to the funds you may need at this time. If you do this, you will need to begin withdrawals by the time your spouse would have turned 70½. The same is true if you were to roll over these funds into an IRA in your spouse's name.

If you wish, you may want to consider rolling your spouse's IRA into a new IRA that is in your name. This is allowable as long as you were the primary beneficiary on the retirement account to start with. You cannot receive distributions from this account, though, until you are 59½, or you will need to pay the hefty pre-withdrawal tax on the funds. The benefit of this is that you get to profit from the money over your own lifespan in comparison to that of your spouse's, which may be helpful in some situations.

In any of these situations, you will need to look at the benefits that affect you personally, which means consulting with your own personal financial advisor first and foremost. You want to be sure that you have all the necessary information regarding your own situation before making a decision like this.

403(b) Retirement Plans

There are other retirement plans beyond that of the 401(k) plan that you should consider looking into. Your employer may offer these plans to you, not giving you another option. With the 403(b) plan, you are offered this if you work with a nonprofit organization and institutions. Good examples include school districts or hospitals. Although there are many people that qualify for this type of plan, only 40 percent of those that qualify actually use it. This is not a good thing, considering the importance of having retirement funds put away every year.

You may hear the plan called a TSA or Tax Sheltered Annuity. In either case, they are an agreement that bonds the employee and the 403(b) provider. The employer's job is very straightforward: They simply withhold the contributions for the employee and send them off to the provider. They do not have any responsibility in the plan. There is no requirement that they contribute to the plan either. It is up to the employee, then, to fund the retirement account, which is one of the reasons many do not set up this account.

There are two ways in which you can contribute to this type of plan depending on how the employer's plan is set up. You can do so under a salary reduction agreement. In this case, you can defer up to a certain amount of your pay into the plan. This method is dependant on how many years you have been with your employer, as well as the current allowable investment limits. Or you can contribute through after-tax contributions. The same maximum amount is in place here.

In a 403(b) account, you have the benefit of tax deferred compounding interest that is so important to developing a solid retirement fund. You also face the same 10 percent penalty if you remove money from the account before you hit the age of 59½. If you happen to switch jobs, you can take the funds to the new company or roll them over into another 403(b) account, into an IRA or other method, but check out the details of the plan. You will find that there are many tricky details that you must know about in this type of plan. One of those is the back-end surrender charge, which will be costly to you. This means that the plan may not allow you to move the funds even if the IRS says it is acceptable to do so. If you do proceed, you could face stiff penalties.

Most withdrawals for this type of account must start by

the time you hit age 70½. If you have contributed money into this account prior to 1987, you have until the age of 75 to begin the process of withdrawing funds. Again, be sure to read the fine print.

There is a contribution limit to these accounts, too. It is the same as the 401(k) contribution limits, and this account will also continue to increase in the allowable amount of deposited funds based on the cost of living changes that are put in place each year.

It used to be that 403(b) plans could only be found as forms of annuities, but this is no longer the case. Now, you can secure mutual fund choices if you would like to. Of course, you should be doing just that. If your organization does not allow or makes it too difficult for you to select the type of fund source you would like, be sure to let your fund manager know. Start a petition with other employees to convince them that you want to have mutual fund choices, too. Usually it will only take a handful of employees to make the change happen.

Legally, you are able to invest your retirement account anywhere that is willing to take the account. You do not have to change jobs if you want to change your plan. Instead, ask about using the 403(b)(7) option. There may be surrender charges that apply, but usually only if you are transferring out of an annuity into a mutual fund. More so, realize that only the amount you have accumulated in savings can transfer, not the contributions themselves.

For those that have had the option of a 403(b) account but have not taken advantage of it, you can use a catch up account to help you get more into your account faster, especially if you are getting older. Your plan provider can help you determine how much, as well as how you can do this. The process requires specific qualifications.

Now that you are investing in your 403(b) retirement plan, the question becomes, "How do I get the funds out of this account?" That can be a difficult situation because moving money out of a 403(b) plan is dependant on that specific plan's goals and the fine print. You will need to read and understand this information. The problem is that, although the IRS allows for rollovers into IRAs from your 403(b) plan, the plan itself may not allow it to happen. If this is the case, you may only have the option of moving your money to a fixed annuity.

When you are 59½, you will be able to begin the process of getting your money out of the account. Before this time, you will need to use what is called Rule 72t. This allows you to remove money from the account in equal payments over a period of time. You will avoid the 20 percent early withdrawal fee if you use this rule, but you must remove money in equal payments each year based on how old you are and how long you are expected to live.

In other words, once you decide to go this route, you must continue to receive the payments for five years or until you reach the age of 59½ or whichever is later. This means that, if you do this when you are younger, you will receive much less per year than you would if you were older. Of course it is also removing money from the account that can no longer grow in value, which will hurt your retirement plan.

If you plan to go this route, it is recommended that you work closely with your professional financial advisor and perhaps a tax professional so that you can make the best decisions for your situation.

457 Retirement Plans

Another option is the 457 retirement plan. These plans are used by employees that work for the state, county, or city. If you are offered this retirement plan, you will be able to defer part of your compensation for employment to these plans. There are different amounts depending on the current allowable amount through the IRS. You can also use a catch up funding option if you have had this type of plan available to you in the past but have not taken advantage of it. This allows you to put in a bit more. Currently, you can defer up to 25 percent of your compensation into this type of fund.

At the age of 70½, you are required to start withdrawing funds from the plan. The money that comes from this plan is considered to be ordinary income and therefore is taxed the same as your paycheck would be. The benefit of this plan is that you get the same tax deferred compounding interest benefit that you would have with other types of retirement plans. But if you decide to take money out before you are 59½ because you are retiring early or because you are leaving your position, you can do so without incurring a penalty. You have up to 60 days to determine what you want to do with distributions from the account.

The problem with this type of situation is that the IRA does not qualify as a deferred compensation plan, according to the IRS. That puts you in a position where you cannot roll over the funds from this account into an IRA rollover if you leave your position. The only other option that you have, then, is to put the money into the same type of 457 retirement plan with your new company. Otherwise, you will be heavily taxed.

SELF-EMPLOYED? YOU ARE NOT LEFT OUT

If you are self-employed, there are a range of options for you to take into consideration. In fact, even if you work full time at a standard job and then work part time in your own business, you have the ability to tuck money away in tax deferred accounts. This is something that is highly recommended, especially if you do not have any other type of retirement savings plan in place.

Remember that as a self-employed person, it will be up to you to set up and manage your account on your own. Although this sounds difficult, it does not necessarily have to be, considering the wealth of options available to you in managing these funds. Having a professional help you with the taxes, legal aspects, and paperwork is highly recommended if you want to be successful.

Nevertheless, here we define several of the options that are available to those that are self-employed but want to provide themselves, and perhaps their employees, with a retirement plan.

SIMPLE IRA: IS IT SIMPLE?

One of the most common options for the self-employed is a plan called the SIMPLE IRA, or the Savings Incentive Match Plan for Employees. This plan is designed to work well for those that have less than 100 employees and offers no other type of qualified retirement plan.

This method is a bit unique in that each employee will have their own IRA, and they can make contributions to it, even as much as 100 percent of their compensation (or up to the indexed amount for that year). You must put some funds into the SIMPLE IRA for each of your participating employees. As the employer, you can elect to put in matching contributions to their IRA or up to 3 percent of the compensation that is paid to the employee. Or you can elect to contribute less at a flat rate; for example, a 2 percent flat rate contribution based on their compensation.

These accounts follow the same basic IRS requirements as other retirement accounts, expect for one key difference: Should the employee determine within the first two years of opening the account that they need to take money from it they face a 25 percent penalty on the removed funds.

The best way to get the SIMPLE IRA accounts set up is to contact and work with a larger mutual fund company or to work with your financial planner. They are not hard to set up, but the legalities and management may be well worth paying someone else to handle. Lastly, these accounts must be set up by October 1st of the first year that you plan to use the plan.

SEP IRAS: ANOTHER OPTION

The next option to consider as a self-employed individual is the SEP IRA. The Simplified Employee Pension plan, as it is defined, is a pension plan that works off the IRA format. This is perhaps the easiest form of self-employment retirement planning you will find. This straightforward plan allows you to select the best managing company for mutual funds and to fill out an application. At that point, you are able to learn how much and how to contribute to the plan. It is that simple.

This plan is favored by many because it is so easy to set up, but is it right for you? As an employer, you must abide by the maximum annual contributions allowable, which currently is 15 percent of the employee's compensation. There is also an annual cap on how much can be considered for that 15 percent in terms of compensation. You can find out what this number currently is at the IRS's Web site, **www.IRS.gov**. These contributions are actually deductible for the year in which they are placed. You can make these contributions at the time that you file your taxes as well.

For those that are considered sole proprietors, the compensation that you can include here can be found on the Schedule C on Form 1040 of your taxes (after deducting your SEP IRA from this number). A sole proprietor is defined as someone that owns and operates an unincorporated business without any other owner or partner in the business.

If you do have employees, they have to be included in this

retirement plan if you are setting it up. They too must be able to receive a contribution percentage from their compensation at the same rate that you select for your own retirement plan. When this is set up, as the employer, you will contribute to their individual IRA accounts. Because they have ownership of these accounts, they can make their own decisions about how the funds are invested. Employees must meet specific qualifications, including being over the age of 18 and having performed services for you and been paid at least $400 in compensation.

These plans work the same as other IRA plans in that they are compounding as tax deferred accounts. They do charge you the huge 10 percent fee if you withdraw money from the account before you turn 59½ years old, though.

KEOGH PLANS

Yet another option for the self-employed is the Keogh plan. This plan offers two options for you to select from, each slightly different. The Defined Contribution Plan is the first, and it is a plan that puts aside a specific amount of income or profit every year for those that participate in the plan. The other is a Defined Benefit Plan. This one sets money aside, determined by the particular retirement goal that you put in place for your future. These are much more expensive to maintain, but they are ideal for the person that is older and behind in their retirement goals. They allow you to put much more money into them, and they work to achieve your specific goals.

The Defined Benefit plan allows for you, as a self-employed individual, to put up to 15 percent of the income into a profit sharing plan (there is an additional dollar amount that is used to determine the maximum amount that fluctuates from year to year as well). In this particular plan, you are able to make changes each year to the percentage that is invested, or you can skip the investment altogether (which is a good thing only when the business is struggling).

The other option is a Keogh plan that is a money purchase version in which you must contribute a specific, set amount per year. This number is set at the time you begin the plan and must be adhered to throughout the time the plan is in place. This is a percentage of up to 25 percent per year of earned income. Eligible employees also must be compensated.

Employees must be included in all Keogh plans. You can set specific requirements for them, such as how old they must be, as well as how long they should have worked for you. These plans also must be reported through the 5500EZ paperwork done annually through the IRS for any employee that is not your spouse and that has total assets of $100,000. This legal requirement is one to leave up to your financial advisor, tax professional, or the mutual fund company that you are working with.

Like other retirement accounts, this one also follows suit in terms of punishing you for taking your money out too soon. Your funds will grow in your account through compounding methods and be tax deferred. If you take the money from the accounts before you turn 59½, though, you will pay the 10 percent penalty on the funds withdrawn, as well as applicable taxes on the funds. If you do decide to leave the plan at some time, you may roll the funds into an IRA account, or you can leave them in the Keogh account if you are leaving the company but want to continue earning interest.

The Keogh account is a good option for many self-employed individuals that want to contribute heavily to their accounts, but the process of setting them up and managing them should be done by a professional, especially if you have employees that are participating.

Note, too, that this type of retirement account is unique in some areas because it is protected from legal judgments and creditors that you have working against you. This differs from one state to the next. Your mutual fund provider can help you determine which protections your state qualifies you for.

THE PENSION?

For those of you that are able to take advantage of the pension, by all means go for it. But, like many other things of the past, the pension is quickly on its way out, as many companies are abandoning it as an option. Still, if you have one, you need to know what they are and how they work for you.

Pension began in the early 1900s but really gained force in the 1940s when unions were being formed and people were demanding better quality working environments and better pay. The pension was the way in which the company promised to provide workers with more benefits even after they retired from the company.

A pension works as a promise from the employer to the employee to pay a specific amount based on various criteria after the employee retires from the company. This future benefit is called a defined benefit plan because it clearly defined what was to be given to the employee at the time of retirement. Usually, only the employer contributes to the pension plan. In the public sector, though, many times employees can also be contributors to the pension plan. That can provide you with a range of benefits because you can add more to the pension as a retirement account. Generally, only state employees have this option.

Pensions work by promising to pay a specific amount per month or year to the employee after retirement. This becomes the defined amounts, but these amounts changed per company and per employee. You may need to meet specific requirements to qualify for the pension, at which time you would be considered vested, or eligible for the full pension benefits offered to you. One common pension requirement was to reach a specific age, such as 62, the retirement age of most companies. The pension also provided additional benefits if you worked with the company for a longer period of time. The longer you were with the company, the more benefits you could receive at retirement, which is an ideal way to keep people working for one company instead of many.

The problem with the pension plan is not for the employee (although he too will suffer in the long run) but for the employer. The employers that use pension plans are spending a small fortune on keeping them up and running. The process of knowing how much to put aside for each employee is quite costly, especially if the person lived longer than expected.

Most companies have done away with pensions partly due to the fact that they are so costly. The company that offers one must hire a professional to determine how much money must be put aside each month to pay for their employee's pensions. To come to a number, they must determine what the expected life span of each employee is and determine how much that employee is costing them. So, if James will retire in ten years, they need to know how much they must put aside today to pay for James's lifetime (and perhaps his spouse's too) to have enough to pay for this. This costly situation is one that many companies strive to avoid.

Some pensions work simply by factoring a percentage of your salary, whereas others would provide a fixed amount. In most situations, determining how much you will get at the time of your retirement from a pension is hard work and requires complex computations to say the least.

The problem with pensions from the employee standpoint is that there is no cost of living adjustment done for them. For example, if you retire with the promise of a $30,000 a year, that is great. But you should realize that it is always

$30,000, no more. This means that, even though inflation at the rate of 4 percent could be eating into that $30,000, there is no way to get an increase. Over time, that $30,000 would have the buying power of much less, even down to a fraction of what it originally was worth. This brings about the situation in which, although $30,000 may seem like enough to live on, it is in no way going to be enough due to inflation.

That being said, some pension plans do offer a cost of living adjustment, but these are rare. People working in the public sector most often have this extra benefit. To find out if your pension plan offers this type of coverage, talk to your human resource manager or the plan's administrator. Do not assume that it is there.

THE RISKS OF COUNTING ON PENSIONS

If you do have a pension, it should be considered in your retirement plan. But it should not be counted on either. The fact is that any and all pension plans can be terminated at any time. There is no governing law requiring that a company has to keep the pension plan in place. In fact, most companies are now switching employees from the costly pension to the more affordably managed 401(k) plans because of the cost to the employee.

Other companies are pushing employees toward different types of plans that offer a combination of the defined benefit plan and the defined contribution plans. One of the common options that some companies are using is called a cash balance plan. This method uses either a percentage of a compensation method or a flat dollar amount to determine the formula for calculating the benefits you will receive. It guarantees a specific rate of interest that the account will earn. Each employee has their own individual account.

If and when you leave the employer, the account can be rolled over into an IRA, or it can be taken with you to another employer that offers the same type of account.

As you can tell, this costs the employer a much lower amount of money per employee, which is why many employers are using this method instead of the pension. More so, they do not have to contribute as much annually in a defined manner.

But how does a company go from point A (pension) to point B? This is where things can get a bit tricky, especially if it is your company that is in the transition. The older employees that have been with the company longest are generally given the option of going for the new plan, while the youngest employees are often more happy to take the newer, non-pension plan. Because they can select, they choose what works best for them. But what if you are in the middle of the transition? This group is the one that loses out because they often are caught in the middle with little opportunity to make the right decision for themselves.

IT IS TIME TO WITHDRAW YOUR MONEY

Now that you have a pension in place, you are expecting a nice big paycheck. How do the IRS and other factors play a role in the withdrawal of the funds from your pension? Most pension plans do not offer a lump sum withdrawal. If it does offer this, take it and move your money into a rollover IRA until you need to use it. The other benefit of rolling it over is that you get to control where the funds are placed in terms of investments.

When you have this opportunity, contact a brokerage company to work with. Look for a company that allows you to make a direct transfer into the IRA. If the employer must issue the funds to you directly from the pension account through a lump sum, the employer is legally required to collect 20 percent of that as a withholding. You must come up with that 20 percent to make up for the difference.

For those that do not have this lump sum option, you will begin to receive a check from your pension when you reach the required age as set forth in the pension plan. This assumes that you have retired from the company at this time. Legally, your spouse is required to be the beneficiary of your pension, meaning he or she would get a share of that pension should something happen to you.

If you do want to use your pension money, there are ways to do so. One of them is to use a life only situation. This requires that 100 percent of your pension is paid out. At the time of your death, the pension stops coming in. The Joint Life option allows you to receive a lesser amount over your pension payout period but provides for a guarantee that at the time of your death, the payouts will continue for as long as your spouse is alive. The third option is called a Period Certain. This provides that you are getting a specific number of payments. If you die before you receive all of them, your spouse continues to receive the rest until the last payment is sent.

SUMMING IT UP

Putting the pieces together is far from simple and straightforward. In fact, most people will experience changes over their lifetime that make it even more complex. Yet, the first step you should make in determining what your options are is to talk to your human resource manager or your employer. Find out what options they have in place for those that are looking for retirement benefits.

Even smaller companies are coming around to the benefits of providing their employees with retirement plans. Congress is very involved with the process, realizing that people will be less dependent on federal aide if they have the ability to put away money on their own. They often offer benefits to the employer that sets up these accounts, too.

If your employer does not offer any type of retirement account, find out why and showcase the benefits it will offer to employees, including incentives to remain with the company. You may find that most employers are more than willing to listen to your needs and concerns, especially when you can find a similar company that will offer the retirement benefits you need.

When you find out what is offered by your employer, get started in the process of investing this way. Retirement plans offer a key benefit to you: They allow you to put away money safely and securely, earning a decent amount of interest, and they allow those funds to be untouched by taxes, at least until they are withdrawn from the account. In addition, they help to provide you with the ability to let your money (even that tax payment) to compound over and over again, gaining considerable money for you.

Over the course of your lifetime, it is likely that you will move from one job to the next and see plenty of opportunities for new retirement plans. You may end up with several retirement accounts, and that is perfectly acceptable. When you combine your collection of retirement accounts with those of your spouse, you may find yourself with a large number.

Nevertheless, to keep track of them all, you should consider putting old retirement accounts into a rollover IRA. You can put them in together or separately, but the goal is to make managing them much easier. Be sure that you know where your money is and how much you have tucked away.

Even though retirement savings accounts like those discussed in this chapter are essential to your retirement plan, they are not all you need. You will not want to touch these funds until you have to, which is often at the age of 70½. Therefore, you need other funds, called taxable funds, to pay for life from the time that you retire until you hit that age. Unless you have three to four million dollars in that retirement account, it is best to leave it untouched until you have to use it. If you get into those funds now, chances are good that you will not have enough left later to take care of yourself.

12

IRAs MUST BE UNDERSTOOD

The IRA, or Individual Retirement Arrangement, is just that. It is a way for people that do not have other means of putting retirement funds aside to do just that. But you can have more than one account. When this method of saving for retirement was first introduced, it was clearly a front runner with consumers because it allowed them to put away a good amount of money that would build wealth through compounding and was not touched by taxes until much later.

In fact, when it was first brought out, you would have been able to deposit up to $1,500 into the account each year. Since that was 1975, the amount would be closer to being about $5,000 in today's dollars. Today, that is not the case, in that the amount you can put into your IRAs is generally much less.

No matter what type of IRA you have, there are annual contribution limits in place that you cannot surpass.

Those limits vary depending on how old you are and what year it is.

In 2007, if you are under the age of 49, you will be able to put up to $4,000 into an IRA per year. If you are above the age of 50, you are allowed to contribute up to $5,000 individually. In 2008, those under the age of 49 will be allowed to invest up to $5,000, and those above 50 will be able to invest up to $6,000. Congress has also put in place the ability for contributions in the future to continue to rise with the cost of inflation in increments of $500.

Your spouse also can contribute to his or her own IRA account. Or, if your spouse does not work, you can contribute to his or her IRA on their behalf. There are many regulations, including the fact that you both must have separate accounts and you must file a joint income tax return. The contribution that you both make should not be more than the taxable amount of compensation you are reporting on your tax return.

If you have not set up and used an IRA to this point, you can use a catch up contribution to help you get more into your account faster. For the years from 2002 until 2005, you can put up to $500 into the IRA for each year. After 2005, up to $1,000 can be deposited as a catch. You can only contribute catch up funds to your IRA if you are over the age of 50. With all catch up payments, be sure to look for the latest information from the IRS or from your financial or tax professional. This information changes, and the investments must be classified properly to avoid fees or problems.

To get the funds into your IRA on time for it to count for the tax year, you must make all your contributions by the deadline of April 15, unless this falls on a weekend. Then it must be on the next business day of the year following the year you are contributing for. To make sure that you take advantage of this to the fullest, be sure that when you submit your income tax return each year by April 15 you have fully funded your IRA account. You will need to record this information on your taxes in most cases, too.

There are many types of IRAs and each offers something unique that you need to consider. The Traditional IRA, which we have discussed thus far, is the most commonly used. The Roth IRA began in 1998, and it provided additional help for those investing in their retirement. This nondeductible contribution offers the same benefits, but the difference comes from being qualified for distributions that are free from federal tax. Nondeductible IRAs were put in place to help those that did not qualify for other types of IRAs, usually because of a different type of retirement option at their place of employment.

IRAs can be so confusing that you should always consult with a professional before making the leap, but, to help you, we have included much of the information you need here.

MAKING SENSE OF CONTRIBUTIONS

IRAs are worth the trouble of learning about their complexities. The first thing to realize is that they are always changing in terms of allowable contributions and who qualifies for them. Congress, the main factor behind these changes, wants to encourage people to save as much as possible on their own, therefore reducing the stresses on public health and funding sources. Just as Congress changes, so do the goals of these various programs. For that reason, make it a point to find out what the latest information and goals are. The best way to do that is to check out IRS Publication 590, which provides all the details you need in a current form. This can be found on the IRS Web site (**www.irs.gov**) under the name of Individuals Retirement Arrangements.

Each of the various types of IRA accounts has a different set of rules that need to be followed. This is why it is so complex. Although we explain much of what you need to know here, doing your own homework may be necessary.

To begin with, what is an IRA? This is an Individual Retirement Account in which you will put personal savings aside to pay for your retirement years. It provides the all important income tax advantages that we have discussed to this point and allows you to compound interest. This makes it something you must take a closer look at.

For an IRA to work, you must contribute funds to it. These funds that you place into the IRA are called contributions. You are able to take an income tax deduction for having your IRA in place, and you can accumulate your savings as a tax free basis, until you begin to pull the funds out. Distributions, which are withdrawals from your

IRA account, are going to be taxed, as would any type of income that you have and during the year that you receive the deduction. Although complicated, these rules are similar to those that we have discussed regarding 401(k) withdrawals.

The retirement age of 59½ still stands in that, if you pull funds from the IRA before this age, you are subject to the 10 percent tax penalty, as well as the income tax charges. There are some restrictions to this that may allow you to withdraw earlier. If you find yourself in a position where you need to withdraw funds (especially large amounts) from your retirement fund before your retirement age, talk to your financial advisor about doing so first. Find out if there is any way to pull funds without triggering this penalty. As you have seen earlier, it can be extremely costly.

On the flip side, you must also begin withdrawals of the money from your IRA by the time you are 70½ years of age. The IRS has made this perhaps the most complicated area in which they govern. The amount that you need to withdraw, the timing, and even the effect on beneficiaries is all very complex and best advised on a per situation basis from a tax professional. The fact is that if you do not begin taking your IRA distributions in time, you could face a 50 percent penalty, determined by what you should have withdrawn and what you did. This is highly costly to your retirement plan, which is why you should plan to begin withdrawals at the age of 70, as discussed in this book.

TYPES OF IRAS BROKEN DOWN

While the IRA is a factor in providing you with a retirement bank, it is one simple tool. There are actually five different types of IRAs that you should take into consideration. Each offers something unique that could be right for you. Here we break down the various options that you have to consider.

The Traditional IRA

The first kind of IRA is the Traditional IRA. Here you can contribute up to a designated limit (see information earlier). This limit, like those previously listed, is subject to change each year.

The amount that you contribute to this IRA is deductible on your income tax return. The amount that is deducted is dependant on the Adjusted Gross Income (AGI) that you have, and if you have a retirement plan from your employer already in place. Some contributions to your IRA will be fully deductible while others will only be partially. Some may not be deductible at all. This depends on your AGI, your filing status, and your contribution amount.

Educational IRA

Another type of IRA is the Educational IRA in which you can put funds away each year at the maximum limit, which can then be used to pay for the education of the beneficiary. For example, if your grandson is just in diapers but you know you want to be able to pay for his college education, you can use an Educational IRA to do so. Here, the funds can be put away and can grow at the same rate as other IRA accounts, including compounding and tax free basis, until your beneficiary needs them. Only authorized educational expenses can be covered by this situation. Although not commonly used, they can work for some people if this is their goal. On the other hand, they are also very specific in who can contribute to such a plan, how the funds can be disbursed, and the level of contributions that can be made.

If you are considering this type of IRA, find out if there may be another option for providing these educational goals that are not as restrictive. Your financial planner can help you with this. Many state-sponsored plans are a better option than the Educational IRA.

SEP IRA: Simplified Employee Pension

We have discussed similar versions of this IRA in the 401(k) section. This is an employer-sponsored IRA. It is a Simplified IRA in that the process and make up is just that — simpler than a pension. The employer can place up to 15 percent of your compensation into this IRA account. Because you own your own IRA account, you have control over how the funds are invested. SEP IRA accounts like this can be beneficial to those looking for a simpler option over the Keogh retirement plan.

SIMPLE IRA

The SIMPLE IRA is another solution to consider. This is

one of the more popular options because of how easy it is to put in place and take advantage of. Your employer will sponsor this plan, and the employer also administers it. This plan offers several benefits. One is that the employer can establish the SIMPLE IRA and contribute to it. The employer can put in place his own plan (which makes this ideal for those that are self-employed) and provide for his employees as well. Secondly, employees also contribute to this plan. Employees can contribute up to 100 percent of their compensation but no more than a set limit per year (currently set at $6,500 per year). This gives you more room in which to maneuver, providing for your own retirement savings and benefiting from the employer's help.

Roth IRA

The Roth IRA is another option, one in which you will find several benefits and a unique spin. In Traditional IRAs, you get a deductible on your income tax for contributing to your IRA. When funds are added to the account, they are done without any taxes. Later, when you pull the funds from the account, there is a tax placed on them similar to income taxes. The idea is to allow your funds to grow over time, untaxed, giving you the most opportunity to see growth. But what if you did not want to pay taxes at all?

With a Roth IRA, this is possible. Contributions that you make to the Roth IRA are not deductible on your income tax, not when you put the funds in and not when you take them out. But the benefit here is that not only do you get to take a tax free break when the funds are going in, but also when they are coming out. They are considered tax free even at the time of distribution.

If you want to qualify for this type of IRA, you will need to meet specific guidelines, including an Adjusted Gross Income that is less than $166,000 if filing jointly. If you are filing singly, your AGI must be lower than $114,000 (these numbers are for tax year 2007 and change yearly). In addition to this, when you place funds into the account, they must stay there for the first five years that you have the account open. If you do try to remove funds at this time, you will face a heavy penalty.

Anyone that qualifies for this type of IRA should set one up and use it to the fullest extent. While you do not receive a tax break on your income taxes, the fact that you do not need to pay tax on the retirement funds even when you take them out means that you will save yourself thousands of dollars in the long run. The money that is growing is completely yours for your retirement.

CHOOSING THE RIGHT IRA FOR YOU

The process of selecting the right IRA for your situation is one that usually comes down to two factors: what is the best bottom line cost benefit to you and do you have a retirement plan at your place of employment.

For those that have retirement plans through their employer, such as a 401(k), you do not qualify for the Traditional IRA. If you are not given this option (or only your spouse is) you may be able to qualify for the Traditional IRA.

Secondly, you need to determine which the best overall choice for your situation is and which will give you the most money.

Let us say that we compare three situations. In situation one, funds are put away for 20 years in a traditional IRA. In situation two, funds are tucked away in a Roth IRA, and in situation three, they are just saved in a taxable account.

What you will find is that each offers a different opportunity for investment and gives you a very different bottom line. To start off, the person that puts funds into a taxable account will make the least money in the long run. That is due to the fact that income tax must be paid yearly on these funds, which will hurt them in terms of growth (there is no compounding of those tax dollars in the account). You would have saved less by far over the other two situations.

Now, the first situation with the traditional IRA offers some benefits. Because it is tax deductible, you are able to save funds and get the deductible, which will help you pay fewer taxes. On the other hand, the second situation allows you to receive no deductible but allows you no taxes later. In the long run, the second situation will save you the most money and cut you down the least amount in taxes. The Roth IRA offers a higher percentage of money in your pocket over the traditional IRA.

This is actually only one benefit of the Roth IRA though. Another is the fact that, if you do not need the funds from the Roth IRA, you do not have to use them. The Roth IRA does not have to be used in your lifetime and therefore is often used as a vehicle of passing funds from one family member to another (although it may not be the best way to do so). The fact is that the Roth IRA allows you to use your funds as you see fit.

Another advantage of the Roth IRA is that it simply does not matter which tax bracket you are in. Because you do not have to pay taxes on these funds, you do not have to worry about the tax brackets at all, which could save you considerably in the long run.

Still, you may make more if you tuck away those tax deductions from the traditional IRA and save them. You may find yourself able to put more away, which would give you extra funds in the long run.

How do you know that the tax deductions you receive with a traditional IRA are not worth it? In many cases, they are not, but you still may want to consider all aspects of each of these. Again, you should work with a professional to help you determine what is right for you.

If you have a plan at work in which you have other coverage for your retirement, we suggest the following goals.

If you make less than $33,000 and are single, go with the Roth IRA if you qualify. If you make between $33,000 and $43,000, put some of your money into both the traditional and the Roth IRAs. If you make between $43,000 and

$114,000, put your funds into a Roth IRA. If you make over this amount, place some into the Roth account and save the rest.

If you are married, things change a bit. If you make up to $166,000, put your money into a Roth IRA. If you make more than this, you will need to put most of your money into the Roth accounts and some into taxable accounts.

Now, if you do not have any type of coverage in terms of retirement plans at your place of employment, you have different options to consider.

If you make less than $40,000 and are single, we suggest putting your money into the Roth IRA. If you make between $40,000 and $114,000, put your money into a Roth IRA and a traditional IRA to gain the most benefit. If you make more than $114,000, put your money into a traditional IRA instead.

If you are married, things change again. If you make less than $62,000, go for the Roth IRA, and if you make up to $166,000, split the funds between both types of accounts. For those that make more than this over the course of the year, the rest will need to be put into a taxable savings account.

So, why do these things? First, realize that if you are in the lower income tax brackets, the tax deduction you receive is 15 percent. That is not going to help you in the long run in terms of what you will pay when distributions start. Moreover, if you do have a plan offered to you at your place of employment, you will have both types of plans available to you at retirement (taxable and nontaxable) giving you much more to play with.

I HAVE A TRADITIONAL IRA, BUT I WANT A ROTH IRA

If you currently are putting your money into a traditional IRA but see benefits in moving your money to a Roth IRA, you can definitely do so. There are several ways to do this. Moving your funds from a traditional to a Roth will allow you to take advantage of the growth that is tax free (not just tax deferred). To move these funds, you will need to use one of these methods.

The most common way to move funds is through a rollover. This is usually done when you leave your place of employment, but can be done at any time. You simply move your funds from your traditional IRA into your Roth IRA. Funds must be moved within 60 days of the closing of one account to remain untaxed.

Trustee to Trustee Transfers is another option. You can instruct the trustee of your traditional IRA to move the funds into a Roth IRA through your Roth trustee. Your Roth trustee is the person or company managing your Roth IRA. You can get the necessary paperwork to make this switch directly from the Roth IRA trustee, and they will help to set up the account for you.

The final way to move money is through a Same Trustee Transfer. If your current trustee also offers Roth IRA options for you, you can keep it with that same trustee.

This method allows you to move funds from your traditional IRA into the Roth IRA without changing companies or trustees. Most trustees do offer both options, and this may be the easiest option for you to use. What really happens is that the trustee simply re-identifies the account as a Roth IRA rather than a traditional IRA. Your money technically never moves, but the distinction is what counts.

When you use the Trustee to Trustee transfer or the Same Trustee Transfer methods, you do not have to sell off all your stocks and bonds to open the new account. Assuming both brokerage firms (if you have two) offer the same types of accounts, there is no reason to sell off anything. Your investments should automatically convert to the new trustee and new account without a problem. The only problem with a Trustee to Trustee transfer may be if the Roth IRA trustee does not offer the same funds that you own in your traditional IRA. The process may take some time to work out, but it should not be a problem in the end. You may want to select a brokerage that offers the same types of funds so that this is simplified on your part and theirs.

There are some limitations on transferring these funds to a Roth IRA, though. You must be married and filing a joint tax return (called a MFJ), and your adjusted gross income must also be less than the allowable amount for that year. If you are married but file separately, chances are you will not be able to convert your traditional IRA to a Roth IRA at all.

If in fact you do make the conversion and you wind up

making more than you are allowed for that year, you will have a failed conversion, which means you will need to quickly move your account back to the traditional IRA. If you see this happening and did not plan for it to do so (such as a large end of year bonus that puts you over), you must work with the Roth IRA trustee to fix the situation; otherwise, you will face huge penalties making the entire process not worth it.

WHAT ABOUT THE TAXES?

For those that are converting from a traditional IRA to that of a Roth IRA, there are taxes to think about, too. When you make this conversion, you will have to pay taxes on all contributions, except for nondeductible contributions. Your regular tax rate applies to these contributions. You will need to report this change on tax form 8606. Usually the entire amount you convert is taxable, but this form will help you determine just how much you will need to enter onto your Form 1040 for the tax year.

One thing to monitor is how much that conversion amount is. If you convert too much into the Roth IRA, you may put yourself into a higher tax bracket, which will cost you considerably. If you do have a large amount to cover, do it over a period of time. Put some of your traditional IRA into the Roth IRA each year until fully converted. If you plan to do this, be sure to use your tax professional to help you get it 100 percent right.

In order to justify converting to a Roth IRA, be sure that the additional tax is from a non-IRA fund that pays for your conversion. In other words, let us say that you plan to convert a sum of money that requires you to pay $5,000 in taxes on it. Do not take those funds from the IRA or any other IRA that you have. Rather, pay that out of your taxable funds. You do not want to sell off anything that would create a capital gains tax either. If you have cash you can use to pay this tax, do so. If you cannot do so, do not convert your holdings from a traditional IRA into a Roth IRA. The reasoning is as simple, as it may not make up for the cost in the long run.

You also have to look at the bigger picture. For example, if you were to take that $5,000 and apply your own savings methods, you may be able to make more money on it than you would by converting your IRA. In addition, you have to consider medical deductions, miscellaneous deductions, and other tax credits that you may qualify for as well.

WELL, THEN, NOW WHAT?

You are likely even more confused today than you were before. To convert to a Roth IRA, make sure that you are considering all these details, even if you are looking for a partial conversion only:

1. You should be sure that you qualify in that year by looking at the current income limits in place for that tax year.

2. Do not make the conversion if your tax bracket is

raised too much and especially not if it pushes you over the 31 percent barrier.

3. Be sure that the funds used to pay taxes from the conversion will come from non-IRA funds, such as from cash or other taxable funds. Do not touch retirement accounts for these funds.

4. You should not need the funds or plan to touch them for at least 20 years. This gives them enough time to grow and be worth the benefits of paying those additional taxes at this time.

There are resources you can use to help you make this decision. The key resource you should have is your financial planner, who can set up both situations for you using computer programs and tell you what the ultimate best decision for your needs is. Needless to say, these can be tricky decisions with complex calculations.

There are also a number of financial calculators out there that you can use before talking to your financial advisor. These can help you see what the overall outcome will be when converting your traditional IRA into a Roth IRA. We recommend looking at all possible situations and find the best decision for your financial situation.

In the end, if a full conversion is going to be too costly, find the ideal number for you in a partial conversion. This allows you to move some of the funds without costing you too much in the long run. You will have some funds in each type of account, which allows you more flexibility at the time of retirement.

IRA DISBURSEMENTS: GETTING TO THE MONEY

Your goal is to hold off on using your retirement income as long as you can. This tax deferred income will continue to grow the longer you leave it in place. Throughout this book we have discussed the importance of compounding interest, which will make the difference for you in the end. In the latter years, the compounding itself will be a huge contributor to the amount of money available to you. The more there is in the account to compound the more you will make.

Nevertheless, most people will need to use their retirement plans to fund some of their retirement. Your goal is to make this happen but not until you reach the age of 70 or so. If you hold out that long and have followed the plans we have discussed, chances are good that you will have plenty of money to take you through the last 30 years of your life. Prior to this time, you should be using your taxable income, including Social Security and pensions that have started.

When you do need to use your retirement income, including that from your IRAs, it is important to know the ins and outs of how to do so and when to do so. Like all retirement accounts, IRAs also disbursement rules that must be followed. Each is a bit different, though, and you should know how to handle this for each type of account you have. More so, you should plan for the costs associated with each method long before you will need to use them.

ROTH IRAS: THE BIGGEST BENEFIT

The best benefit of the Roth IRA is that you get to withdraw money from this account tax free. You put the money in without paying taxes on it, and when you take it out, there are no additional taxes to pay. This is the beauty of this IRA structure and the reason why we encourage you to use this method.

The other benefit we have mentioned about the Roth IRA is that you do not ever need to touch these funds if you do not want to. Let us say that you have so much put away that you never need to tap into these funds. Unlike other accounts, the funds here are yours to pass down and to leave to whoever you want. Your spouse does not even need to use this Roth IRA, if he or she elects to use the Roth IRA as his or her own.

More than likely you will need to use these funds, though. Remember that you must leave the funds in the account untouched for at least five years; otherwise, you will be charged fees. After the passage of that fifth year, you can begin qualified distributions if you meet the requirements. Those requirements are any of the following.

- You are 59½ years old and want to take disbursements now.

- You are disabled and therefore need the funds.

- You pass away, at which time the funds are disbursed to your beneficiary.

- You and your spouse qualify as first time home buyers.

For the last of these, it is essential that you work with your financial planner to determine the best way to access your funds. A mistake here could be quite costly to you or to those that receive your retirement money.

Also, if you have a Roth IRA that has been converted from a traditional IRA, realize that the conversion date is the start of the five required years, not the original time frame that the traditional IRA was set up. Also, if you have more than one Roth IRA, each has its own five-year period from the date that it was created.

What if you need to pull funds out and they are not considered qualified disbursements? If this happens, you face a 10 percent penalty, as we have mentioned. You also must pay the necessary taxes on those disbursements, which means that, even if you have a Roth IRA that offers no taxes assessed at the time the IRA is set up, you still must pay them if you do not take qualified disbursements.

There are some exemptions put in place to help those that must do this to avoid paying high taxes on their money. For one, if the withdrawals are considered part of a series of substantially equal payments, you may be able to avoid the tax structure. If this is the case, you must continue to withdraw these amounts over at least five years and until you hit the age of 59½. Any change to this plan causes you to become liable for paying the 10 percent tax penalty. Plus, you must pay interest on the withdrawals that have been made up until that point.

To determine what amount you are able to withdraw, you should work with your financial advisor or brokerage firm. There are three different methods that can be used to calculate this, all of which are complicated and all of which can offer different amounts that may suit you better.

If you have large medical expenses that must be paid and you do not receive reimbursement for them, you may qualify to have the taxes lifted. This also applies if you are paying medical insurance premiums because you have lost your employment. If you owe the amount to the IRS because of an IRS levy on the plan or if the amount is less than the qualified education expense you pay that year, you can also pull funds from the Roth IRA without paying tax penalties on the funds.

For anyone that needs to withdraw money from their Roth IRA early, before the age of 59½, it makes sense to first talk with a tax professional about doing so. He or she will help guide you in the right direction and also will help you avoid as many taxes as possible.

If you are doing this, you may want to consider why. If it is because you have run out of money because you retired early, perhaps you should not have retired at all. The fact is these funds are meant to help you much later in life, and if you do not have them put away for that time, you may find yourself struggling later. Make significant headway on these accounts so that you do not need to touch them and are not tempted to do so.

TRADITIONAL IRAS: GETTING TO YOUR MONEY

Traditional IRAs are a bit different than the Roth IRA. As you now know, there are taxes to pay when the funds come out of the IRA. Many of the same qualifications exist for the traditional IRA. To withdraw funds from your account before you turn 59½, you still must meet the same qualifications as listed for the Roth IRA. Again, we urge you not to do this, as it seriously injures the value of your IRA.

If you need to take a disbursement and you meet the criteria for doing so, you will not have to pay the tax penalty of 10 percent. Otherwise, you will have to do so. In either case, you still must pay income tax on these funds when they are released no matter when they are released.

When you are 59½, you can begin to take the disbursements from your traditional IRA without penalty. The amount you withdraw can be anything that you want or need it to be. The taxes levied here are at the same tax rate that applies for everything else, except for nondeductible contributions. These are contributions that you filed with the IRS on tax form 8606. When you turn 70½, (or by April 1 of the year following this age) you will need to take the required minimum distributions, called RMD, from the traditional IRA each year. If you do not take the required amount, there is a 50 percent fee charged to you. This is the difference between what you need to take and what you have taken.

Do not wait until April of the following year. If you do, you will be required to take two required minimum distributions at that time. One will need to be taken by April 1st and the other before December 31st, which may put you into a higher tax bracket for that year because of the two payments. Instead, take one when you turn 70½, in that same year, so that you are only taking what you must. This helps keep those funds in your hands rather than paying 50 percent of it to the IRS as a penalty tax. A good way to do that is to try and take that first disbursement three months before you turn 70½.

REQUIRED MINIMUM DISTRIBUTIONS: WHAT IN THE WORLD IS THAT?

The RMD the IRS requires you take out of your IRA each year after you turn 70½ is a large, important factor for you to take into consideration. Remember, this is the amount of money you must take out of your IRA each year. If you do not withdraw this money, the difference between what you did take out and what you should have is subject to a 50 percent penalty. You must know how much you need to remove and when if you are to avoid this.

The rules all changed in 2001 when new laws helped outline how this process was to happen. The fact is that the IRS determined that their older laws, dating back to 1987 were simply "too complex" and "too restrictive." Many feel that they simply were too restrictive and it was too difficult for even the IRS to make sense of it all. Nevertheless, the new laws have made it simpler, though not less harsh, for you to determine what amount of money must come out of your IRA each year.

The law changes also help the taxpayer take out less than they had to before without being subject to the same taxes. If you have income from your taxable accounts, this is good news because now you do not have to touch nearly as much from these accounts as you would have. After all, the longer those funds sit there, the more valuable they become for you and that means success in building your retirement dollars even farther.

There are three life expectancy charts used to factor in these qualifications the most common of which is called the Uniform Lifetime Table. This chart can help you determine what your required minimum distributions should be. That chart is listed on the next page.

To use this chart, you need to find your age, or the age of the retired person that owes the IRA. Find the corresponding distribution period. Divide the IRA's value by the distribution period from this chart. This is the person's required minimum distribution. This number is the amount, in dollars, that must come out of the IRA to forgo the tax penalty of 50 percent.

Here is an example: Louis is 75 years old. He has an IRA that has $650,000 in it. According to the chart below, his distribution period is 22.9. This means that this year Louis must remove at least $28,384 from his IRA to forgo the taxes on it.

If he only takes out $20,000, the penalty of 50 percent is put on that additional $8,384 that he did not withdraw, meaning that he has to give the IRS a check for $4,192. That is money that simply did not have to go to the IRS. If he would have simply pulled out the additional funds and put them elsewhere, he could have saved that money for later in life.

REQUIRED MINIMUM IRA DISTRIBUTIONS					
Age of retiree	Distribution period (in years)	Age of retiree	Distribution period (in years)	Age of retiree	Distribution period (in years)
70	27.4	86	14.1	102	5.5
71	26.5	87	13.4	103	5.2
72	25.6	88	12.7	104	4.9
73	24.7	89	12	105	4.5
74	23.8	90	11.4	106	4.2
75	22.9	91	10.8	107	3.9
76	22	92	10.2	108	3.7
77	21.2	93	9.6	109	3.4
78	20.3	94	9.1	110	3.1
79	19.5	95	8.6	111	2.9
80	18.7	96	8.1	112	2.6
81	17.9	97	7.6	113	2.4
82	17.1	98	7.1	114	2.1
83	16.3	99	6.7	115 +	1.9
84	15.5	100	6.3		
85	14.8	101	5.9		

Remember too that the IRS does not require this payment to be made in the same manner as the Roth IRA. If you have the Roth IRA, you do not have any required minimum disbursements and therefore this table does not apply to you.

If you have a spouse who is much younger than you, by

at least 10 years, this table should not be used. Instead, request that the Joint Life Expectancy Table be used. Doing so will help you stretch out your income even longer to account for your spouse's longer life expectancy. The spouse should be listed as the sole beneficiary on your IRA in this case. You can find this table and more information on it in the IRS's Publication 590.

Also, when you pass away, beneficiaries need to be taken into consideration. If you name more than one beneficiary be sure you realize that your beneficiaries should sort out your IRA to give them the best tax avoidance abilities possible.

Throughout this chapter you have learned the ins and outs of IRAs. Realize that they are one of the best ways for you to put money away for your retirement years. Remember these key points about them:

- Choose the right IRA that fits your needs and your lifestyle.

- Stay up to date on the changes that often happen with these IRAs. You will need to monitor any and all changes that happen in regard to how much you can invest in your IRA and how much must come out. This information is readily available from your financial planner and through the IRS.

- Leave your money there. The penalties for withdrawing your money from the IRA are far too costly. When you begin investing, it may not seem like that big of a deal. But time is the best builder of wealth. In later years, compounding at such high numbers will produce incredible results.

If you have not started an IRA yet, now is the perfect time to do so. Add funds to it monthly to make it easier to manage. Or put your tax return into your IRA every year. Whatever you do, get one in place today.

13

YOUR ESTATE PLAN

We have talked about many ways for you to plan for the later years of your life. The plan is simple: Spend the next years of your life building wealth in taxable and nontaxable accounts. Use your taxable accounts for the first years of your retirement. Use your nontaxable accounts after you turn 70 to fund the remainder of your life. It should work quite well.

But what happens when you leave something behind? Although you are planning to live to the age of 115, perhaps you will die when you are 110. What will happen to the funds that you had set aside for those remaining years? As part of your early retirement plan, you should put an estate plan in place, which will provide the protection and coverage you need to have in case things do not go as you planned.

The delicate balancing act of having enough money to outlive you but not having too much to leave behind is difficult. Enter the tax man who will try to claim as much of your estate as possible. You need to make decisions now to protect it. The good news is that you can protect virtually every aspect of your retirement income, as well as any assets you have from the tax man.

We recommend developing a thorough estate plan, and you will want to dedicate a fair amount of time to doing so. Excellent resources exist that will help you make this happen as well. Your goal, then, is to develop a good relationship with your financial planner and work on developing a working estate plan. Life will change from today until the day you are ready to retire and will change throughout retirement. For this reason, a working estate plan is necessary because it will allow you to make changes as you see fit.

If you are married, you and your spouse should be protected if one of you dies early or if you both die young. If you have young children, an estate plan can provide protection for them if something should happen to you. Your assets can all be planned for and cared for if and when you are not there to care for them. You can care for your pet, provide for your long-term health care needs, or even fund your grandchildren's education. An effective estate plan takes care of everything you want it to during your life time, as well as after you are gone.

IS A WILL GOOD ENOUGH?

Many people think their final wishes will be included in a

will and read by their attorney. While wills are commonly used and are helpful to some degree, they are not often the best estate plan for you. Consider the will an important first step, but not a final document.

Your will should include several key elements to help define the most important goals for your estate when you die. This includes the following:

- It should list guardians for your children that are still minors. This should be something that is thoroughly understood by the guardians themselves. Although morbid to think about, it is necessary to consider what protections and considerations you want to provide for your children if you cannot do it yourself. Your wishes for your children are always strongly considered by the courts, but the court will still determine if it is the best choice for your children and make that final decision.

- It should name an executor or several co-executors of your will and estate. This will be the person that puts all of your wishes into motion. This person should be told about this and agree to the responsibility long before you write down their name. It is a huge decision, and often the best person for the job is someone that you trust that is slightly removed from the situation, such as a friend.

- Identify any specific considerations and requests that you have, defining what it is, and why and how it should be honored.

Your will should be witnessed. You should have it properly structured, too, because mistakes can lead to your wishes being discarded, although this is rare. Your attorney should be the one to write it out, finalize it, and have it properly witnessed. When developing an estate plan, it is essential to hire a professional attorney to help you. He or she will provide you with the highest quality service and often can help with all your retirement goals.

Your will should be revisited at least every five years until you reach retirement age and when a major change has happened. Major changes happen all the time. For example, you should make changes to your will if you move to a new state, have another child, get divorced, see an increase or decrease of significant size in your estate, or when you change your mind about your desires. Also, laws that could affect your will continuously change. Having an attorney that is up to date on these changes will help protect your will as well.

THEN THERE WAS PROBATE

Perhaps the largest and most troubling aspect of your will's success will be probate. Probate is the legal process that your estate must go through at the time of your death. Essentially, the courts take control of your estate. Their goal is to pay off all your debts with your assets, and then take what is left, which is heavily taxed, and divide it among your heirs. They do honor your will, but they also have the final say in how that will is executed. All this is done through your will's executor. Your state's laws will direct the process of probate. Every state has a unique set of laws to do just that.

Your will's executor will do all the work. It is his or her job to find all the assets that you list, to pay your bills, and then to divide up your estate as you have defined.

Probate watches and monitors how the process is going and if it is being done according to the letter of the law. Having your attorney working with your executor is a good decision since the legalities of the process can be difficult for anyone to manage. Make sure that your attorney is a specialist in estate planning and probate so he or she can provide you with the best experience in creating an effective will that is approved by probate and that is easily executed.

If you do not put a will in place, the state's probate court will assign an administrator of your estate. That person will then make all decisions regarding where funds should go and how your estate is broken down. It is essential to keep the decisions in your own hands or at least those of your trusted family and friends rather than a court appointed person.

RIGHTS OF SURVIVORSHIP

An area that you should take into consideration is the rights of survivorship. Any assets that you and your spouse both own should have a "joint tenant with right to survivorship" clause to them. This means that, when you die, your property goes directly to your spouse and therefore does not go through the probate process.

Community property laws are in effect for nine states only — Arizona, California, Louisiana, Nevada, New Mexico, Idaho, Texas, Washington, and Wisconsin. These states require that any and all property purchased when you are married becomes community property between you and your spouse. That means that all that property is half owned by you and half owned by your spouse.

Your will can dispose of your half of the property, but that means the half that is yours must go through probate at the time of your death. This can draw things out for quite some time if, for example, your spouse wants to sell the home after you have died.

What if you devise your will to not provide much, if anything, for your spouse? As your spouse, he or she has the right to "elect against the will" in most states. Most states provide that spouses must be given an adequate inheritance. In most cases, this is at least a third of the assets that enter into probate.

When it comes to owning property as a couple, it is essential to know the best way to do so. For example, for those without a lot of assets in their name, the best thing to do is to have property owned through joint ownership and with the rights of survivorship. This makes the process of keeping those assets with the surviving spouse very easy to manage.

But this is not always the best situation. For example, if you get married a second time, what should be done to take care of your children from your first marriage? You must also take into consideration the taxes your estate will go through.

THE PERILS OF ESTATE TAX

It is highly recommended that you plan for your death as soon as you begin to accumulate any type of property or wealth. If you do not, estate tax could cut into the value of anything you leave behind.

Any property you have that is jointly owned between you and your spouse is easily passed from the deceased spouse to the surviving spouse. Your spouse does not pay any taxes on that property because of the Unlimited Marital Deduction law.

But when the second spouse dies, things change considerably. Now, an estate tax must be considered because the full value of the estate is levied for taxes. This can be a considerable amount of money given to the government. However, this does not have to happen in many cases.

The Unified Federal Estate and Gift Tax is the tax law to focus on. This is a transfer tax on large estates. This tax is one that poses taxation on anything you give away during your lifetime or even after your death. The value of those items must be taxed. Estate taxes and gift taxes have the same tax rate, which is why they are lumped together.

Estate taxes are levied on property that is over the yearly allowable value of your estate. Once you go over this threshold of value, your property becomes subject to taxing. Your goal is to be sure that the value of your estate that enters probate is less than this estate tax threshold. Can you make that happen? Yes, and the best way to do so is to use one of the various options of dividing your property before you die so that it can avoid probate altogether.

By doing this, your property passes from you to the heirs without consideration for probate. No probate means no estate tax is levied on the property. Not all property can pass this way, but you should get as much as possible through using this method so that you can keep your estate under the required amount, which, for the year of 2007, is $2,000,000. This amount can change yearly, and it has been rumored that Congress is trying to phase out the estate tax altogether.

METHODS TO AVOIDING PROBATE

There are several ways you can avoid probate. The larger your estate is, the more important it is to do this. Start by knowing where your larger estate pieces are located and determine what you would like to do with them. When you can move them into a safer, probate free situation, you will be able to protect your estate in the long run.

If your estate is valued lower, you may be able to skip probate court altogether. This is not always the case, and since you are planning to retire early, chances are good that your property will be valued highly, making it likely to pass through probate.

Instead of looking for a way to get out of the estate tax, avoid it altogether. Move property out of your will and into another financial vehicle. Doing this can save you thousands of dollars because you do not have to worry about the estate tax. Your heirs will thank you for that because they will wind up with much more of your hard-earned money. Unless you want to give it to the government, consider these options.

Joint Tenancy

If you are married and plan to stay that way, joint tenancy is the best route to take. If you plan to allow your spouse to have your assets after you die, you must label those assets as joint tenancy assets. It is also the most straightforward method of protecting yourself.

In some situations, you may be charged a gift tax for leaving your property to your spouse if he or she is not listed as being a joint owner of the property. This can levy just as much tax. If possible, look into another option that will give you more reassurance.

Your estate planning professionals (your lawyer and your financial planner) can help you determine the best route to take in this situation. You definitely want to consider the benefits of this option compared to others you have.

Living Trust

A living trust may be one of the best tools to use to protect your property from probate and still protect your heirs, too. This tool gives you a good amount of protection and control over your property. Even if you should become incapacitated, you will still have protection and control over what is in your estate (at least that which is mentioned in your living trust).

A living trust allows you to put property into the trust and allows you to manage it as you see fit, but that avoids probate court. There is a downside to this situation, though. These trusts are difficult to create, which means you will need the help of your estate planning attorney. The cost of hiring a professional to do this work for you is well worth it because it will protect a large portion of your property from estate taxes.

The living trust requires attention. You will need to make decisions regarding virtually every aspect of that trust on a regular basis. Should you make changes to your decisions, you must change your living trust to match it. What is more, this can become costly, especially when you are managing your trust over a long period of time. We firmly recommend considering the benefits of a living trust, though, and implementing it as a form of managing your estate after you are gone.

Solutions That Are Specific

There are other solutions to consider. These are specific to the type of property you want to pass down to your heirs. For example, you can use a Transfer on Death Car Registration to pass your car to your heir without it having to move through a probate court.

Securities you own are likely to be one of the largest considerations you have, especially since you are building these rapidly to care for your later years in retirement. They too can often be protected. A Transfer on Death Registration for Securities is available in all states except for Texas. This will move your securities to the person you list on the transfer notice at the time of your death. This is quite an easy and affordable way to move your securities without having to go through the costly probate process.

Yet another solution is a Transfer on Death Deed for Real Estate. If you own property, this may be an ideal solution for you. This will allow you to move property to your listed beneficiary quickly at the time of your death. This tool is not available in all states, but if it is allowable in your area, it is well worth investing in.

Beneficiary Account Set Up for Qualified Accounts

In many of your accounts, you can set up beneficiary terms when you create them. This can be changed later if necessary. For example, in a pension plan, the income you will be receiving after you retire can be funded to your beneficiary after you die. That means that your income is still coming in to take care of your spouse or other family without having to wait on probate to sort it all out. This can be greatly important for many people. With pensions in particular, there can be stipulations on which differ from one plan to the next. Read through the pension documents to find out what protections are provided to your heirs.

Since we have dedicated much of this book to your retirement accounts because you will be spending so much of your life building them up, the last thing you want is for them to go through probate court where heavy taxes are levied on them. The good news is that when you set up any and all of your retirement accounts, you name a beneficiary that will receive the proceeds from your plan at the time of your death. For example, your IRA or 401(k) plan is protected from probate because you are able to list who you want to take control of it after you die.

Another thing to quickly think about here is your life insurance policies. We recommend having them in place until you are no longer caring for dependants. These policies pay out at the time of your death and can be life savers for your family members that are struggling to maintain the bills without you. Life insurance policies do not go through probate either.

Other Solutions for Avoiding Probate

A few more solutions exist. One of them is Tenancy by the Entirety. This type of plan is only available in locations where there is common law; however, only a few states are considered common law states. This is a good option for moving property from one spouse to the next, but it is only going to work for those that are not at risk of becoming incapacitated or of having their marriage dissolve. In those cases, probate is used to determine the best solution for your property.

Pay on Death Bank Accounts are a consideration for some, too. These accounts can be set up through your bank in the same way other accounts are set up. They are simple, straightforward methods of saying where the funds in that account will go at the time of your death. This method may work for some of your government securities, as well as bank accounts you have. The person listed as the beneficiary of these accounts will receive the ownership of the account when you die. This solution only works for those that want their funds to go to adults, not children.

OTHER CONSIDERATIONS FOR YOUR ESTATE PLAN

Your estate plan should be created with the help of a financial planner, someone that will work closely with you to make sure your goals are met after you die. It is incredibly important for you to determine what those goals are and the best way to make them happen. Here are some things to take into consideration when planning your estate.

What do you want to provide for in your estate plan?

This should include educational goals, charities that you want to help fund, and any specific people you want to take care of. Your estate plan can do anything you want it to if it has the right legalities behind it. We suggest writing down those goals that you want to accomplish and then working with your attorney to make them happen.

What about your wishes for yourself?

For many people, the estate plan can help provide for their wishes in terms of their own care. If you become disabled to the point of being unable to communicate your wishes and needs, it can be extremely important that you have those issues addressed beforehand. No one wants to believe something will happen to them, but the possibility always exists. In addition, be sure that you and your spouse sit down and talk about all these decisions ahead of time. Your estate plan and will can dictate what you want to happen in terms of long-term care, resuscitation directives, and much more.

Who do you want to take care of your affairs?

Your estate plan should clearly identify someone as your power of attorney and when he or she is needed. For example, if you were to be involved in an accident and are unconscious, your power of attorney can and should be used to make decisions for you. This person should be someone that will make decisions for you, not for themselves or the wishes of others. It is imperative that you list this person's express duties.

Your estate plan should fit in with your goals regarding money, life, and health. It should display virtually all your goals for the last years of your life. What is more, you must come back to that will and estate plan often and be sure that it is targeting your situation at the current moment.

Estate planning can help you make sure your goals and your money are taken care of after you are no longer able to do so yourself. As part of planning for your retirement, an estate plan will also offer you the ability to monitor the successes of your plan.

CONCLUSION

This book provides you with ways to meet your goals. With this help, you will clearly be able to meet your goals and retire early. The process does take a long time to make happen, and right now you may feel overwhelmed for sure. Yet, with the right goals in mind, you can make it happen.

Start by understanding where you are today. What are you doing today to make your goal of early retirement happen? Chances are that, by reading this book, you have a good idea of what you need to be doing. You need to pay down your debts and increase your savings. From here, you should concentrate on finding the right professionals to help you create your investment plans and your retirement savings. Those two elements are the backbone of any successful retirement plan.

Work with your employer to find the best retirement vehicle for you and for them. Or, if they do not offer any help in this field, go for an IRA plan that does not require employer contributions. There are so many investment plans that can help you, and there is certainly one that will fit your goals perfectly.

Make decisions in your every day life that help encourage your goals of retiring early. Gone are the days when you can count on pensions from an employer and Social Security to fully fund your lifestyle. You will want more when you retire and that means planning for it now. The end result is that you will be readily able to meet your goals if you are able to make smart decisions about your money today.

Be frugal in your spending. Cut back where you can so that you can ultimately put more money away. Your goal should be to put at least 20 percent of your income into investments, savings, and retirement plans. Chances are good that you will spend half of your life in retirement (especially if you retire early) and that means having the funds to support yourself. You must make decisions based on one question: Is having this item or experience now going to mean more to me than retiring early means?

If not, perhaps those funds should be used to pay for your retirement instead of the immediate gratification. The process of saving enough to fund retirement is less about having more income and more about using what you have wisely.

Can you make your dreams come true without investing? You may be able to do so, but you may not be able to retire as early as you would like to, and it will require putting much more into savings. The strategies we have put in place here for you do not show aggressive growth. We know that your money is important to you and that increasing your risk level will not allow you to comfortably invest in your future. But you should not need aggressive growth strategies if you can work on your retirement with moderate growth investments. You do not have to expect huge returns if you want to retire early. You just have to invest wisely.

Use the resources you find in this book to structure your future. Plan to retire early by making the right decisions with your money today. What will you do with your retirement years? Will you spend your time enjoying your life on the beaches around the world? Will you instead enjoy funding your grandchildren's education and being able to watch them grow up? Perhaps you just want to live comfortably, enjoying each day.

There is little reason to believe that you can have these things if you do not start planning for your retirement today. Start today at achieving your retirement goals. Start today at finding the professionals that will guide you and hone your abilities to make early retirement something that you no longer have to dream about.

The solid and quality plan this book provides to you is your key, your answer to retiring early. The process is incredibly simple for you:

1. Reduce debt, spend wisely.

2. Work hard to save at least 20 percent of your income.

3. Invest hard but not aggressively in a well producing fund.

4. Contribute to your retirement plan at the highest level that you can without being taxed on it.

5. Hire professionals to help you guide your investment decisions.

By doing all these things it will allow you to see the real growth that is available to you. It will allow you to develop a financially sound approach to your life. Your retirement years be successful and enjoyable and so will all the years you spend working toward this goal. After all, you will be financially well off starting today.

Are you ready to dream your dreams and create the path to achieving them? You can do so starting today by implementing change into the way you live. You do not have to give up your life style to achieve your goals. In fact, all you have to do is commit to making wise decisions with your money. If you start today at the age of 30, 40, or even later, you can put yourself in a position to be financially secure and living the retirement that you want sooner than you think.

To get started, we leave you with an expense chart so that you can more easily see your current financial situation and prepare for the future.

EXPENSE CHART			
EXPENSE	CURRENT COST	INFLATION RATE	COST AT RETIREMENT
Housing	$		$
Real Estate Taxes	$		
Utilities	$		$
Maintenance	$		$
Car Insurance	$		$
Homeowner's Insurance	$		$
Housing Association Fees	$		$
Food	$		$
Clothing and Personal Care	$		$
Auto Expenses	$		$
Travel Expenses	$		$
Entertainment	$		$
Pet Expenses	$		$
Gifts	$		$
Hobby Expenses	$		$
Health Care	$		$
Additional Expenses	$		$
Total Expenses	$	x	$

To calculate expenses, multiply the current expense total by the amount of inflation to get the total.

BIBLIOGRAPHY

- Brock, Fred. *Retire on Less Than You Think: The New York Times Guide to Planning Your Financial Future.* New York, NY: Henry Holt 2004.

- Carlson, Robert C. *The New Rules of Retirement.* Hoboken, NJ: Wiley, 2005.

- Clyatt, Bob. *Work Less, Live More the New Way to Retire Early.* Berkeley, CA: Nolo, 2005.

- Lee, Dee and Jim Flewelling. *The Complete Idiot's Guide to Retiring Early.* New York, NY: Penguin 2001.

- Silbiger, Steven. *Retire Early? Make the Smart Choices.* New York, NY: Harper Collins, 2005.

AUTHOR DEDICATION AND BIOGRAPHY

To my husband and children, who have helped me to create the life I've dreamed of living.

Sandy Baker is the mother of three and the wife of an amazing man. Together they provide a range of helpful tools to help others to make their dreams and wishes come true. Estate planning is part of the tools that Sandy helps to present to others as a method of enriching their lives through leaving their legacy. With many years of professional writing experience, namely as a ghostwriter, she's written and researched the topic for many years, enhancing her ability to provide a thorough book for readers.

GLOSSARY

Adjusted Gross Income (AGI): The amount of your income that determines when and if IRA contributions can be deducted. It is calculated by taking your AGI from Form 1040A or Form 1040 and adding back certain items such as foreign earned income, housing deductions, or both; student-loan interest, tuition, and fees; excluded qualified savings bond interest; and excluded employer-provided adoption benefits.

Balloon Payment: a lump-sum payment due at the end of a loan. Balloon payments are usually structured as part of a short-term loan, sometimes referred to as a bullet loan. A bullet note can be written either of two ways. The most common requires periodic payments through the term of the loan, followed by the final balloon payment. Alternatively, the payments can be deferred to the end of the term, at which time the borrower pays the balloon payment, covering both interest and principal.

Blanket Mortgage: One mortgage that uses two or more properties to secure a real estate-backed note. If the borrower fails to pay back the loan according to the terms of the note, the lender has recourse against all of the property securing the loan.

Capital Gain: The net profit realized from the sale of a capital asset (stocks or real estate, for example). Taxes on capital gains are paid at a different rate from regular income, depending on how long the asset was owned.

Cash on Cash Return: A calculation often used for analyzing return on real estate investments. It is computed by dividing net income by the total cash invested (cash on cash ROI = net income + cash invested).

Collateral: Property used as security against a loan.

Excess Accumulation: The portion of a required minimum distribution (RMD) that is left in the traditional IRA account instead of being withdrawn. A 50 percent penalty applies to excess accumulations.

Excluded Individuals: Parties with whom your IRA is specifically prohibited from transacting business.

Excluded Transactions; IRA investments and business transactions specifically prohibited by the IRS.

Fiduciary: A person or institution with a special relationship of financial trust or responsibility to others.

Foreclosure: A legal procedure taken for the purpose of terminating a property owner's rights, usually due to default on a note for tax obligation.

Junior Note: Any note that is secured after the senior note. There can be any number of junior notes, but only one senior note. In the event the borrower defaults of the loan, the holder of a junior note can file a claim for payment, but the claim will be paid only after the senior note is satisfied.

Modified Adjusted Gross Income (MAGI): MAGI is calculated by adding back in certain deductions, such as foreign income, student loans, and IRA, that were subtracted to establish the adjusted gross income. MAGI is used to determine eligibility for IRA deductions and Roth IRA participation.

Primary Market: When you sign a note directly with your lender, the transaction is said to take place on the primary market.

Real Estate Investment Trust (REIT): A business enterprise established for the sole purpose of buying, managing, and selling real estate holdings.

Required Beginning Date: The year in which required minimum distributions must begin, typically 70 1/2, although it can vary in the case of an inherited IRA.

Rollover IRA: A traditional or Roth IRA that holds assets that originated from an employer-sponsored retirement plan.

Secondary Market: When one lender sells a note to another lender, the transaction is said to take place on the secondary market.

Senior Note: A secured debt that will be paid first in the event of a foreclosure.

Short Sale: A real estate transaction where the sales price falls short of the outstanding balance on the mortgage.

Special-needs Beneficiary: Any individual who needs additional time to complete his or her education or requires ongoing special care due to physical, mental, or emotional condition.

Sport Price: The current market price for a commodity such as precious metals, petroleum, or agricultural products.

Tax-Advantaged Account: A savings account, such as a 401(k) or IRA, which receives favorable tax treatment by the IRS. The IRS requires that rollovers from an employer plan go directly into another employer - sponsored plan. But once they are co-mingled with your other IRAs, you lose that flexibility.

INDEX

Retire Rich With Your Self-Directed IRA: What Your Broker & Banker Don't Want You to Know About Managing Your Own Retirement Investments

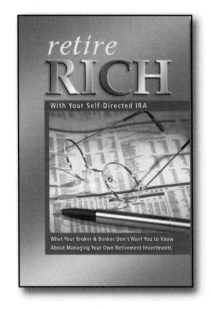

Recently investors have exited the stock market because they have lost control. They relied on the advice of brokers and financial advisors and retirement accounts have dwindled or not increased. There is a great alternative: the self-directed IRA. Learn how to turn your IRA into a wealth-building tool that you control! Find out how to benefit from new IRS rules and stay away from problems. With a self-directed IRA you can purchase real estate, buy a business, invest in tax liens, stocks, bonds, mutual funds, or any investment allowed by IRS regulations. This book shows you how to set up your account with a custodian to deal with the day-to-day activities, such as depositing contributions and settling transactions. It's easy and puts you back in control of your retirement.

ISBN-10: 0-910627-72-X • ISBN-13: 978-0-910627-72-6
288 Pages • Item # RRI-02 • $21.95

To order call 1-800-814-1132 or visit www.atlantic-pub.com

The Complete Guide to Planning Your Estate: A Step-by-Step Plan to Protect Your Assets, Limit Your Taxes, and Ensure Your Wishes Are Fulfilled

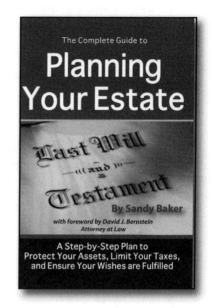

This book explains the complicated issues, terminology, and planning strategies of estate planning. Topics covered are wills, assets, settlement costs, probate, guardianship, executors, life insurance, living trusts, living wills, durable power of attorney, catastrophic illness, potential long-term care needs, martial deductions, types of trusts, federal and state estate exemptions, charitable remainder trusts, power of attorney, avoiding tax on life insurance, gift tax issues, generation skipping transfer tax, and much more. Estate planning should be a positive experience. It involved reviewing your situation and planning for your future. Advance planning is a way to show your love and reduce potential distress later.

ISBN-10: 1-60138-049-6 • ISBN-13: 978-1-60138-049-4
288 Pages • Item # PYE-01 • $24.95

To order call 1-800-814-1132 or visit www.atlantic-pub.com

DID YOU BORROW THIS COPY?

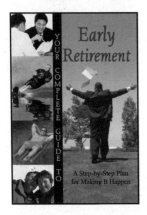

Have you been borrowing a copy of *Your Complete Guide to Early Retirement: A Step-by-Step Plan for Making It Happen* from a friend, colleague or library? Wouldn't you like your own copy for quick and easy reference? To order, photocopy the form below and send to:

Atlantic Publishing Company
1405 SW 6th Ave • Ocala, FL 34471-0640